First-Time
Quiltmaking

learning to quilt in six easy lessons

Landauer Books

First-Time Quiltmaking

learning to quilt in six easy lessons

This book was designed, produced, and published by Landauer Books

A division of Landauer Corporation

3100 NW 101st Street, Urbandale, IA 50322

800-557-2144; www.landauercorp.com

President/Publisher: Jeramy Lanigan Landauer
Director of Operations: Kitty Jacobson
Editor in Chief: Becky Johnston
Project Editor: Linda Hungerford
Art Director: Brian Shearer
Contributing Technical Advisor: Janet Pittman
Technical Writer: Rhonda Matus
Technical Illustrator: Linda Bender
Editorial Assistant: Debby Burgraff
Photographer: Craig Anderson Photography
We also wish to thank the Stitchin' Mission™ first-time quiltmakers
for sharing their quilts made with love for charity.

Library of Congress Cataloging-in-Publication Data

Johnston, Becky.
    First-time quiltmaking : learning to quilt in six easy lessons / (Becky Johnston, Linda Hungerford).
        p. cm.
    ISBN-13: 978-1-890621-97-1 (alk. paper)
    ISBN 10: 1-890621-97-8 (alk. paper)
    1. Patchwork. 2. Quilting. I. Hungerford, Linda II. title.
TT835.J6374 2006
746.46--dc22

                                            2006040825

This book printed on acid-free paper.
Printed in China
10-9-8-7-6-5-4

                                            ISBN 10:   1-890621-97-8
                                            ISBN 13: 978-1-890621-97-1

six easy lessons

lesson one beginning basics 8

Discover how easy it is to get started in quilting with an illustrated guide to the simple tools and supplies you need to have on hand. For fun fabric shopping, take along photos of actual fabrics that show you the basics of pattern, color, and value and how to use a focus fabric for inspiration.

lesson two preparing the fabric...................20

Pre-washing and pressing the fabric is a breeze. Use the quick-step guide for straightening the fabric. Follow step-by-step photos and safety tips for using a rotary cutter and mat to cut the fabric into strips for piecing.

lesson three sewing accurate seams 32

With a few quick tricks and tips for sewing an exact quarter-inch seam, all the seam allowances that make up your quilt top will be accurate.

lesson four assembling the quilt top............38

For a quick start and flawless finish, choose from three easy quilt patterns—four-patch, single-patch, and three-rail—each sized just right for a 36 x 48" kid's quilt or wallhanging. Then use the techniques you've learned to take the three-in-one quilt challenge—a 42 x 54" quilt combining the three basic patterns complete with corner squares and inner and outer borders.

lesson five making the quilt sandwich 70

Making a quilt sandwich is as easy as it sounds. Follow the helpful tips for choosing batting and placing it between the quilt top and the backing fabric. Use pin-basting to hold the layers together until you secure the sandwich with yarn ties or simple machine quilting.

lesson six finishing the quilt 88

Finish by machine sewing a continuous strip of binding around all four edges of your quilt sandwich to cover the raw fabric edges and then hand-sew the binding to the quilt back. Follow easy instructions for adding a sleeve for hanging, if desired. Then, personalize it with a label and you've successfully finished your first quilt!

glossary of quiltmaking terms..........................104

introducing first-time quiltmakers.....................106

gallery of first-time quilts 108

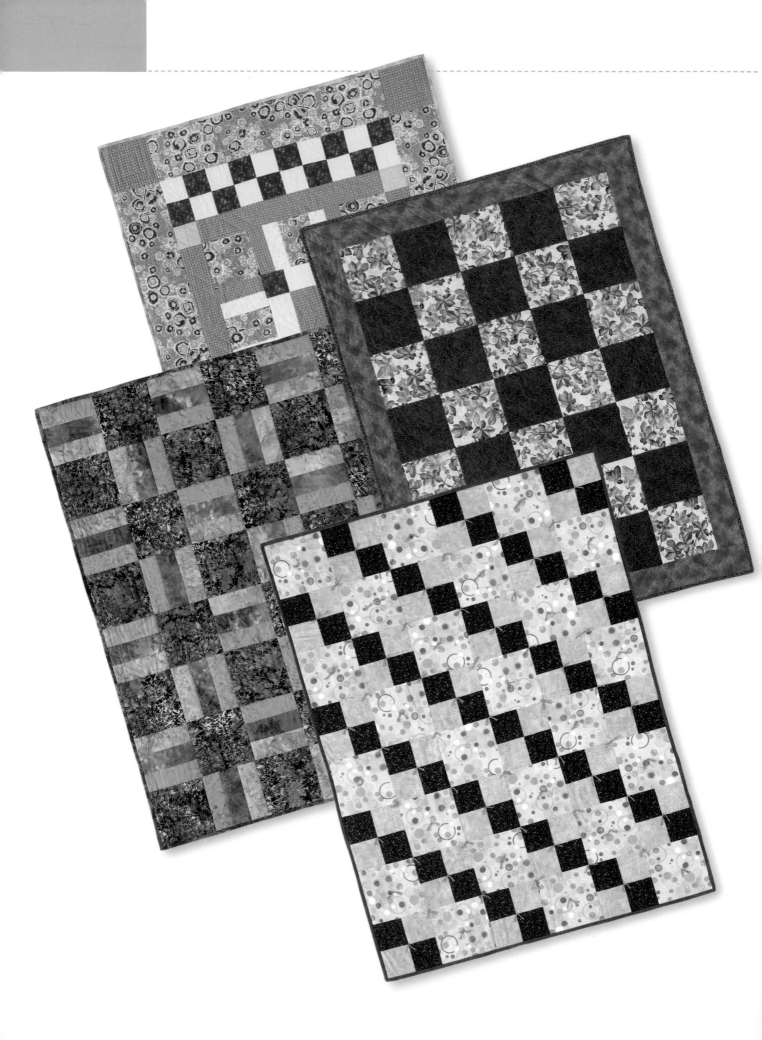

how to use this book

Can you make your first quilt simply by reading through the pages of this book? The answer is a resounding yes! Have you learned how to ride a bicycle...how to swim...how to drive a car...how to bake cookies? Then you can learn to quilt! With basic sewing know-how, a few simple tools and supplies, and a positive attitude you'll soon be saying, "I made this quilt!"

On the following pages, you'll find step-by-step instructions and corresponding photos and diagrams for learning to quilt in six easy lessons using an easy teach-me/show-me format that won't overwhelm you with TMI—"too much information."

In **lesson one**, *beginning basics* will show you how easy it is to get started in quilting with an illustrated guide to the simple tools and supplies you need to have on hand. Shopping for fabric is fun when you know exactly what fabrics to choose for your first quilt.

In **lesson two** you'll breeze through *preparing the fabric* with tips and techniques for pre-washing, pressing, and straightening the fabric. Then follow step-by-step photos and safety recommendations for using a rotary cutter and mat to cut the fabric into strips for piecing.

In **lesson three**, with a few quick tricks and tips for sewing an exact quarter-inch seam, you'll be *sewing accurate seams* for the fabric strips making up your quilt top.

In **lesson four**, *assembling the quilt top* will be fast and fun when you choose from three easy quilt patterns—each sized just right for a 36 x 48" kid's quilt or wallhanging. Then take the three-in-one quilt challenge by combining the three basic patterns.

In **lesson five** *making the quilt sandwich* will be as easy as it sounds with helpful hints for choosing the batting and then layering, basting, and securing the layers with yarn ties or simple machine quilting.

In **lesson six** *finishing the quilt* you'll find it as easy as adding the binding, an optional sleeve for hanging, and a personalized label.

For first-time quiltmaking—whether you're learning to quilt in six easy lessons by going solo or inviting a friend to join you in "Let's help each other" sessions—you can point to your first quilt, and say, "I made it!"

what is a quilt?

A quilt is quite simply three layers of cloth which have been sandwiched together and secured by yarn ties or simple stitches:

A TOP LAYER (the quilt top) made up of individually shaped pieces of cloth joined or "pieced" into a geometric or random design by hand or machine.

A FILLER LAYER (usually batting) that creates the raised motifs on the quilt surface when it is compressed by ties or stitching.

A BOTTOM LAYER (the backing) can be a whole piece of cloth or several fabrics joined together.

Quilting has a language of its own, but getting familiar with a few terms will take you from start to finish on your first quilt. The diagram on the opposite page shows basic terms that will be referred to in the pages that follow. You'll find brief definitions of these and other frequently used terms in the Glossary on page 104.

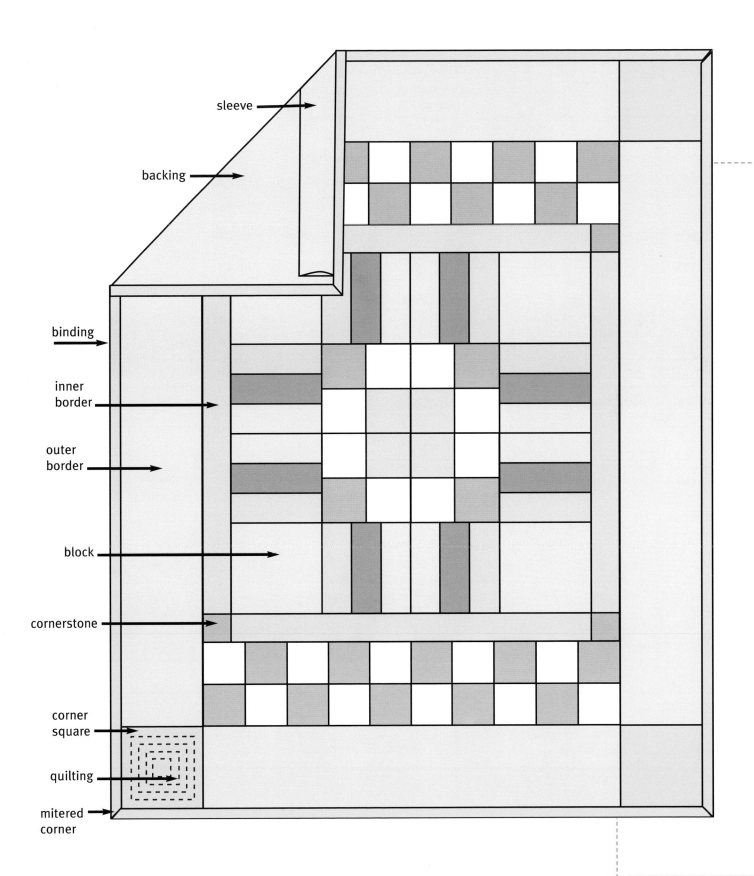

sleeve

backing

binding

inner
border

outer
border

block

cornerstone

corner
square

quilting

mitered
corner

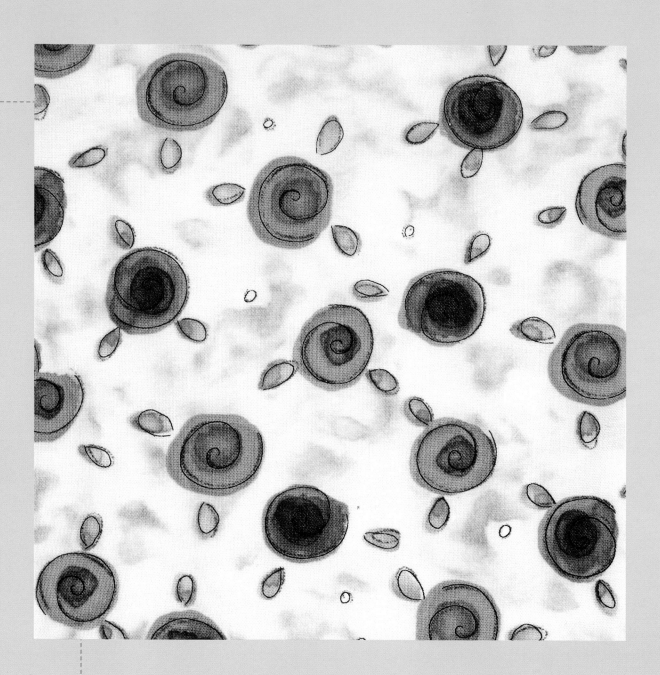

lesson
one
beginning basics

what you need to have on hand

For beginning quiltmaking, you'll need a few tools. A sewing machine and and iron are essential. Whether or not you invest in a machine with all the "bells and whistles," just make sure the machine you use sews an accurate straight stitch—the only stitch beginning quiltmakers really need. Then, get to know your sewing machine. Practice making routine maintenance yourself, and take the machine to a professional for regular maintenance check-ups.

Gather additional quiltmaking tools and supplies either by borrowing from a friend, or making a purchase. If you intend to pursue quiltmaking, working with the proper tools will ensure that your quilts will turn out well and you'll enjoy the entire process.

Use an iron for ironing the uncut fabric and pressing seam allowances.

Make friends with your sewing machine! Read the sewing machine manual to learn how to install a bobbin and needle. Make sure your machine is lint-free, using a brush or soft cloth, and oiled.

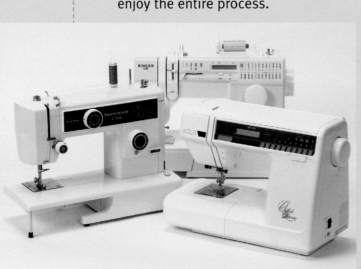

You'll need a sewing machine—old or new—in good working order.

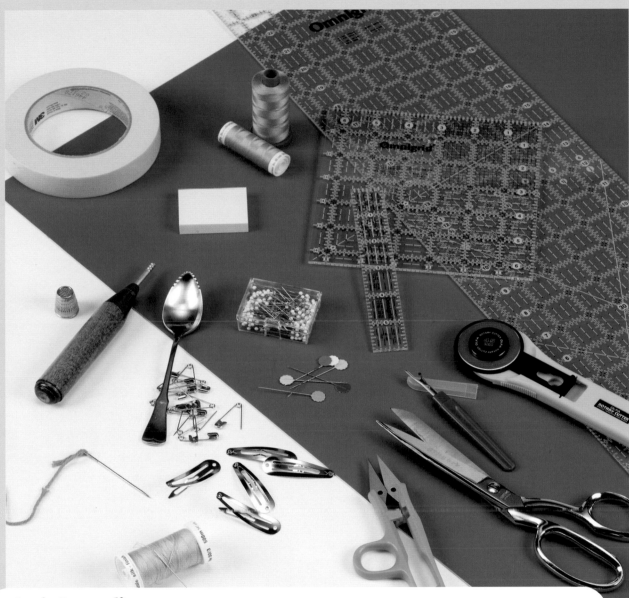

tools & supplies

From top, clockwise shown on a large rotary mat:
- Masking Tape
- Thread (for machine sewing and piecing)
- Rulers: 6-½ x 6-½";
  6-½ x 24"; 1 x 6"
- Rotary cutter
- Seam ripper (for feeding fabric under the presser foot, and for re-working)

Scissors

Snips (for thread clipping at the sewing machine)

Metal hair clips (for temporarily holding binding in place)

Hand sewing needle and thread (for sewing binding)

Darning needle, size 14 to 18, with yarn (for quilt tying)

Safety pins: nickel-plated 1" to 1-½" (for basting)

Grapefruit spoon or Kwik Klip™ (for closing safety pins when pin-basting)

Thimble

Post-it® notes: 1-½ x 2" (for marking a ¼" seam allowance)

Straight pins (flat or round heads as shown in center)

what you need to know about fabric

The best fabric for quilt making is 100 percent cotton. It's easy to cut, easy to sew, and holds up well to handling during and after quiltmaking. Avoid polyester fabrics and polyester-cotton blend fabrics, at least until you become comfortable handling fabric. Polyester tends to pill, is slippery, and can be stretchy, making it difficult to manipulate.

Shopping for Quality

How can you know what the fabric content is for sure? Fabric usually comes from the mill in long lengths folded in half and wrapped around a cardboard core. The finished product is called a bolt. Fabric is unwrapped from it and almost always sold in ¼-, ⅓-, ½- or 1-yard lengths. Information about the fabric is printed on the label at the end of the cardboard core. It is here that you'll find the key ingredient: 100 percent cotton. Not all 100 percent cotton cloth (or fabric) sold in stores is created equally. Though a fabric pattern may appear the same, the milling process for creating the woven goods onto which a design is printed may not be the same—which will be reflected in the price per yard. Two main factors in determining the price per yard and the quality of fabric you buy will be your budget and the quilt's final use. Choose higher quality fabrics for a quilt that will hold its color and strength through many years of use and washing.

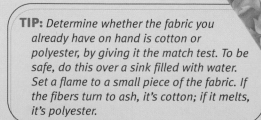

> **TIP:** Determine whether the fabric you already have on hand is cotton or polyester, by giving it the match test. To be safe, do this over a sink filled with water. Set a flame to a small piece of the fabric. If the fibers turn to ash, it's cotton; if it melts, it's polyester.

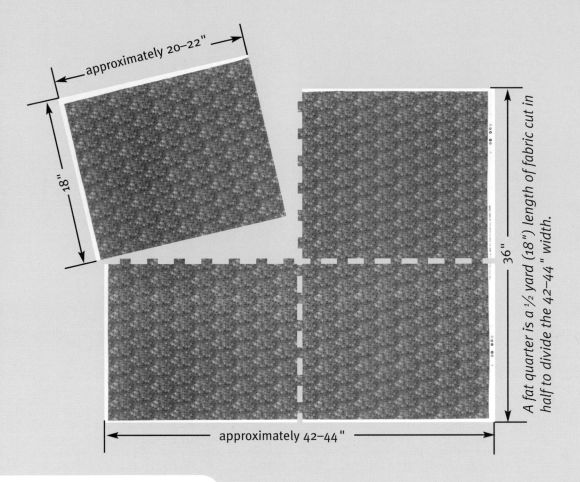

approximately 20–22"

18"

36"

A fat quarter is a ½ yard (18") length of fabric cut in half to divide the 42–44" width.

approximately 42–44"

Starting Small

Start small with fat quarters. One of the quilting terms you'll hear most often is fat quarter or fat fourth. What is a fat quarter? It's a one yard length of fabric that has been cut into four equal rectangles that measure approximately 18 x 20". By making a small investment in pieces of fabric such as fat quarters, you can try out various combinations of patterns. After you've experimented and gained confidence in your fabric selections, you can invest in larger quantities of fabric purchased by the yard.

Adding to your fabric stash

Stored fabric is called a stash. Collect as much fabric as you wish; this kind of stash is legal!

When your fabric stash has every color of the rainbow, but you still need to make a trip to the fabric store for the exact color you think you must have, you'll know you're a real quilter.

what you need to know about selecting fabric

The fun begins when it's time to choose fabrics for your first quilt. All you need to know are a few of the basics of pattern, color and value. In the next few pages you'll find enough information to get you off to a great start. It is also helpful to know how to identify the grain and the bias of fabric.

Identifying Pattern

For an attractive quilt, the key factor is that the scale and type of print used for the fabric pattern provide plenty of interest. Fabric patterns are usually described as small scale, medium scale and large scale as shown below.

Thanks to modern fabric milling, there are literally thousands of choices for types of prints to use for your first quilt—ranging from abstract to directional as shown in the examples opposite.

scale

small   medium   large

print

tone-on-tone

floral

abstract

geometric

pictorial

directional

linear

repeat

novelty

TIP: *We suggest that first-time quiltmakers avoid directional prints—plaids, stripes, and other prints with a linear design. While these patterns add interest to a quilt, beginners may be dissatisfied with how the plaid or striped designs are ultimately aligned—or most often, not aligned! Save plaids, stripes, and other linear type prints for future quilt projects.*

scatter

Choosing Color

Choose fabrics for your quilt based on color cues around you: your favorite colors; nature's sunshine, blue sky and green grass; or images from books or magazines that inspire you.

Warm colors are in shades of yellow, orange, and red. Cool colors are in shades of blue, green, purple. Most colors can be described as warm or cool as shown below.

warm

Establishing Value

Value is the lightness or darkness of a color. Value describes color as it appears in a black and white photograph. As you make your fabric selections, you'll see that their values are relative to each other, depending on how they are placed in a quilt.

light

cool

dark

Finding Focus

We recommend that as a first-time quiltmaker you begin by finding a favorite focus fabric. It's also known as inspiration fabric or feature fabric. A focus fabric can be a novelty print such as animals, sport items, floral or leaf designs, and all types of characters, or a pictorial print.

The focus fabric you choose should have at least three different colors.

Successful quilts have variety and contrast in the pattern, color and value. Once you've settled on a focus fabric, be sure to have it in hand as you choose additional prints with similar colors that include differences. Choose colors that don't necessarily match the focus fabric colors. Select coordinating prints with differing scales and values.

Aim for visual variety because if your prints are too similar to one another, your quilt will look "mushy."

Excellent examples of focus fabrics each featuring three different colors are shown below.

focus fabric

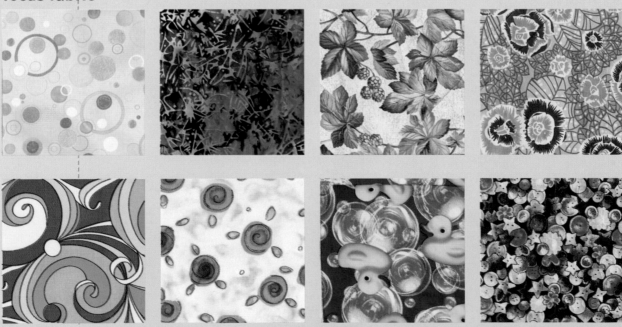

Recognizing Grain

While the fabric you purchase still has selvage and before beginning to handle or cut your fabric, it's helpful to be able to recognize and understand its basic characteristics. Fabric is produced in the mill with identifiable grain, or direction. These are: lengthwise, crosswise, and bias.

The lengthwise grain is the direction that fabric comes off the milling machine, and is parallel to the selvage. This grain of the fabric has the greatest strength.

The crosswise grain is the short distance that spans a bolt's 42" to 44" width. The crosswise grain, or width of grain, is between two sides called selvages.

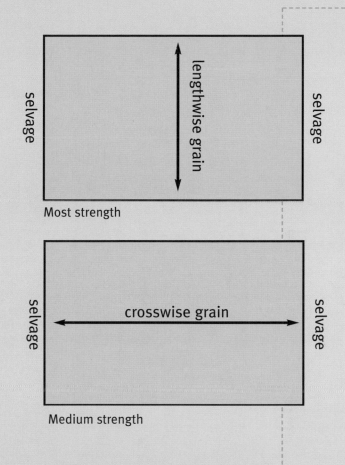

Most strength

Medium strength

Avoiding Bias

Bias is fabric's 45-degree angle and is the direction with the most stretch. First-time quiltmakers should avoid sewing on the bias until they're comfortable handling fabric. With practice and careful handling, bias edges can be sewn and are best for making curves.

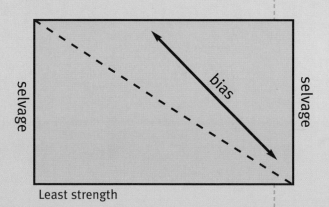

Least strength

lesson
two
preparing the fabric

what you need to know about preparing fabric

A frequently-debated issue is whether to wash or not to wash fabrics before sewing them into a quilt. Opinions are divided, but we recommend pre-washing if time permits.

Pre-washing the Fabric

To pre-wash fabrics, sort them by color, and wash just as you do your regular laundry. For fewer wrinkles, hang fabric to dry. Or, remove fabric from a dryer while still slightly damp.

Press the fabrics right away if you plan to start cutting soon. Otherwise, store the fabric until you're ready to cut into it and press the fabric just before cutting to ensure the accuracy of measurements.

If you make a habit of washing all your fabrics before they're added to your quilting fabric stash, then when you're ready to cut into it you'll never ask yourself, "Have I washed that fabric yet?"

Fabric that HAS NOT been pre-washed...	Fabric that HAS been pre-washed...
requires less handling. Start cutting and sewing it as soon as you bring it home from the store.	is less likely to bleed when the quilt is eventually washed. Washing away the excess dye now helps set the colors and can save future headaches. (Imagine discovering upon washing a finished quilt that the fabric has permanently bled onto other fabrics.) Colors most likely to bleed are red and dark blue.
used on the front and back of a quilt will shrink at the same rate (2% to 3%) when a finished quilt is washed. This results in a quilt with an attractive puffiness around quilting, a look and characteristic that many quilters desire.	is now pre-shrunk (2% to 3% shrink rate), providing assurance that when it's time to wash a quilt, the quilt will not shrink further or unevenly.
handles well. A new fabric's crispness and body can make cutting and piecing easier for a first-time quiltmaker.	has had any surface finish or stiffness washed from its fibers, making it easier to quilt. Quilters who like the crispness and body of new fabric because it's easier to work with, restore it after washing by spraying the fabric with sizing or starch while pressing.

what if:

You've pre-washed all your fabrics and at the last minute decide you need to go to the fabric store to purchase a another fabric to include in your project. If you fail to pre-wash the newest fabric purchased, keep in mind that now you're making something with both washed and unwashed fabrics, and the additional fabric may not be colorfast when you wash the finished quilt.

TIP: *To test your fabric for colorfastness, wet a piece of the fabric and a small piece of white fabric. Place them on a paper towel and allow them to dry together. Check the white fabric for bleeding. If a fabric bleeds, set the color, using equal amounts of white vinegar and hot water, or purchase a commercial brand of color-setting solution. If the fabric's color fails to set, use the fabric with caution.*

Pressing the Fabric

Pressing is vertically lifting up and pressing down an iron, not sliding an iron across fabric as when ironing. Ironing fabric can create distortion that causes misshapen strips and blocks. Get in the habit of lifting your iron up and down whenever you're making a quilt.

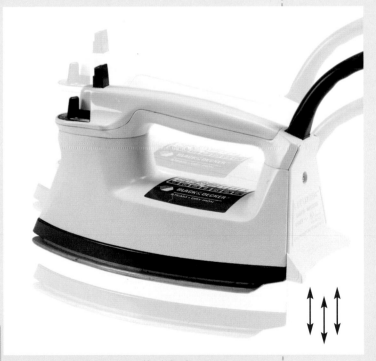

TIP: *Quilters appreciate working with fabric that has a little more body. If you've washed your fabrics, use spray starch while pressing to restore body.*

To press fabric, vertically lift the iron up and then press it down. Repeat this motion for all phases of pressing.

Essential tools for rotary cutting include a mat, a rotary cutter and several rulers.

what you need to know about cutting fabric

Rotary cutting is a quick-cutting method for making fabric pieces. It's easy because modern rotary cutting tools have been designed just for it.

For accurate quick-cutting fabric, we recommend that you begin by purchasing the following:

- a large self-healing rotary mat (at least 18" on one side)

- a 6-½ x 6-½" rotary cutting ruler

- a 6-½ x 24" rotary cutting ruler

- a 45-mm or 60-mm rotary cutter (it looks like a pizza cutter)

> **TIP:** *With a black marker, write "used" on the outside of a rotary blade container. Store several old blades until you're ready to discard them.*

Using a Rotary Cutter

If your rotary cutter does not automatically retract, protect yourself from an accidental cut by habitually sliding the blade protector into place, each time you set aside the cutter.

A NOTE OF CAUTION—ROTARY BLADES ARE EXTREMELY SHARP!

A new rotary cutter blade is extremely sharp but can dull quickly. Before replacing it with a new one, try cleaning it and turning it over. Carefully disassemble the rotary cutter, keeping the parts in sequence. Use a soft cloth to wipe the lint from both sides of the blade. Turn over the blade and reassemble. Once again, handle blades with caution!

Starting with a Mat

Always rotary cut fabric using a rotary mat to protect your work surface. Unprotected surfaces will be permanently scarred, and you'll dull the rotary cutter blade.

Use rotary mat's gridlines only for positioning fabric. Do not depend on the rotary cutting rulers for accurate measurements. The gridlines on the mat may not be accurate, and with repeated rotary blade passes gridlines can become distorted.

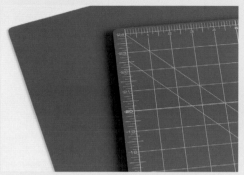

Either side of a rotary mat can be used for rotary cutting. For accurate measurements use rotary rulers instead of the pre-printed lines.

Positioning the Fabric

Use two rulers to cut a straight edge from which all other strips are cut. You'll need the 6½" square small ruler and the 6½ x 24" long ruler. Here's how to do it:

Fold the fabric through the crosswise grain to make the selvages meet. Then, hold the fabric upright to make sure the fold is flat, and the selvages are aligned.

Note: If you only have a 6" ruler, turn to page 28 for an alternate method.

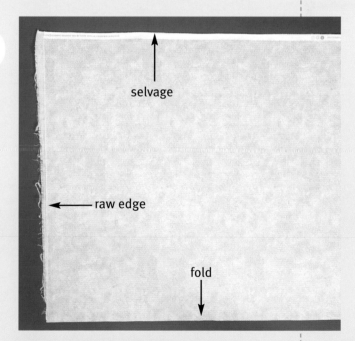

selvage

raw edge

fold

Lay the fabric flat on the rotary mat, with the selvage edges aligned at the top and the fold at the bottom. Note that this fabric's raw edges are not straight; the left edge needs to be straightened.

Use the small square ruler as a guide for positioning the long ruler.

Begin rotary cutting at the fold, always rolling the cutter away from you.

Straightening the Fabric

Lay the fabric on the rotary cutting surface, preferably with the folded edge toward your body. Smooth the fabric, keeping the selvages aligned.

1. Lay the small ruler along the folded edge, placing one of the marked ruler lines on the fold, and the left side of the small ruler near the fabric raw edge as shown in Photo 1.

   Place the long ruler beside, and to the left, of the small ruler, butting them together smoothly. The right edge of the long ruler should lay against the left edge of the small ruler.

2. When the rulers are aligned with the fabric fold as shown in Photo 2, pull away the small ruler, keeping your left hand on the long ruler to hold it in position. The long ruler should be positioned so its right edge is inside the raw edge of the fabric. Make sure both fabric layers of the folded fabric will be cut.

3. Hold the rotary cutter vertical, and with steady pressure, roll it along the right edge of the long ruler, from the bottom to the top as shown in Photo 3.

4. As the cutter rolls, "walk" the fingertips of your left hand upwards across the surface of the long ruler, maintaining pressure to hold the ruler in place while the rotary blade pushes against it as shown in Photo 4.

When the rotary cutter reaches the top, the raw edge of the cross grain has been cut and straightened.

Don't move the fabric! At this point, adjustment to the fabric can disturb the perfect alignment of the cut edges of the fabric.

Quick-Step: Fabric Straightening

- Work from the left raw edge of the fabric
- Align the small ruler along the bottom fold
- Butt the right side of the long ruler to the left side of the small ruler
- Slide away the small ruler
- Rotary cut along the right side of the long ruler
- Roll the cutter as your fingers "walk" steadily from the bottom to the top
- Don't move the fabric
- When you've successfully cut away the raw edge to make a straight edge, you're ready to cut strips according to your pattern instructions.

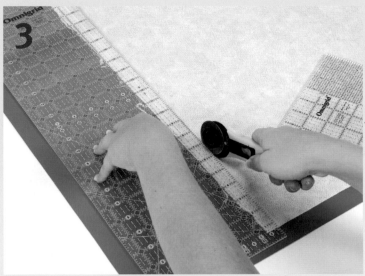

"Walk" your fingertips, rolling the rotary cutter parallel to your fingers.

Roll the rotary cutter in a vertical position making sure the blade does not tip to the side.

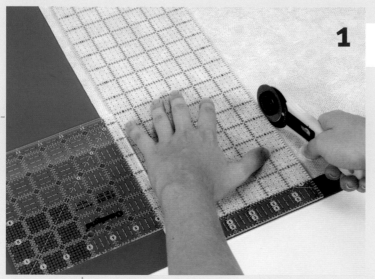

1

If you have only a 6"-wide ruler, use two rulers to measure 6-½".

Measuring Options

To cut a 6-½"-wide fabric strip without access to a 6-½"-wide ruler, use two 6" rulers to measure and cut a 6-½" fabric strip.

1. Use your small, 6 x 6" ruler to measure ½". Butt the 6"-wide long ruler against the square ruler as shown in Photo 1. Together, they total 6-½".

2. Rotary cut along the 24" length of the long ruler.

what if:

If the ruler moves while you're rotary cutting, you may need to cut a new straight edge. It's important to make the cut edge as straight and accurate as possible.

If you didn't apply enough pressure to the rotary cutter to cleanly cut through both layers of fabric, use your rotary cutter on those places.

If you placed the fabric too near the left end of the mat, and the long ruler tipped off the edge of the mat, reposition the fabric so the entire long ruler is firmly positioned on the mat for cutting.

Strip-Cutting the Fabric

Cutting fabric into strips, also called strip-cutting, is most easily done with rotary cutting tools. First straighten the left edge of the fabric according to instructions that begin on page 25. Then, use the 6-½ x 24" ruler and the rotary cutter to cut fabric strips in the width needed for your quilt project.

1. Use the long ruler to measure the appropriate strip width. As when straightening the fabric, align the ruler marks with the fabric's left edge, start at the bottom fold, and roll the rotary cutter toward the selvages, along the right side of the ruler as shown in Photo 1.

Each of the four simple quilt projects featured in Lesson Four uses the same technique to cut the fabric strips, though the quantity and width of each strip varies according to each quilt pattern.

1

Use a piece of masking tape on the ruler as a reminder of the fabric strip width you're cutting—this strip measures 3-½".

TIP: *When repeatedly cutting strips the same width, it is easy to mis-measure. Ensure that the same strip width is cut by placing a temporary, "reminder" mark along the ruler line. Use a piece of masking tape or highlighter tape to indicate the appropriate line.*

Restraighten the left edge of the fabric after three or four strips have been cut.

Re-Straightening the Fabric

After several successive cuts, strips will become slightly crooked from the distortion caused by the rotary cutter and from a ruler that's even a hairline off the mark. Fabric selvages may also become unaligned.

1. To restraighten, refer to page 26 to realign the selvages. Cut the left edge of the fabric and continue to cut strips as shown in Photo 1.

You might find it helpful to turn the fabric around and straighten the opposite end—a great way to neaten any leftover fabric that goes back into your stash.

Expect to restraighten the left edge of the fabric after cutting three or four fabric strips.

You may need to completely open and refold the fabric, then restraighten the left edge before continuing to strip-cut.

Fabric strips may look like this after four or more cuts have been made without restraightening the left edge. Notice the "elbow" that begins to form in the center.

Sub-Cutting the Fabric

When the fabric strips for your project have been cut, you're ready for sub-cutting each strip into a smaller size using the rotary cutting rulers and the rotary cutter.

1. Begin by straightening the left edge of the fabric strip to remove the selvage as shown in Photo 1.

2. Use the small square ruler to sub-cut the fabric strip into smaller units as shown in Photo 2. These will be the squares, rectangles and border strips you'll use for assembling the quilt top for the projects featured in Lesson Four.

Always begin sub-cutting the fabric by straightening the fabric strip's left edge. Here the selvage is removed.

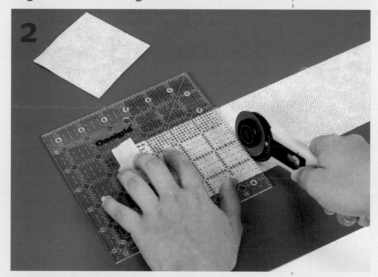

Use the small square ruler to sub-cut a 3-½" fabric strip into 3-½" squares. Note that masking tape is used as a quick visual guide to indicate the measurement on the ruler for the 3-½" square.

lesson
three

sewing accurate seams

what you need to know about sewing accurate seams

The keys to sewing accurate seams are the size of the sewing machine needle, the thread used for the needle and the bobbin (the round case which holds the second thread).

Choosing Needle Size

For piecing fabrics together on your sewing machine, use a size 70/10 or 80/12 sharp sewing machine needle, or an 80/12 universal needle. Note that sewing machine needles are available in European and U.S. sizes. As an example, for the sewing machine needle recommended above, the larger number (70) is European; the smaller number (10) is U.S.

Choosing Thread Weight

Choose a 50- or 60-weight, two- or three-ply 100 percent cotton thread for the sewing machine— threaded through the needle, and in the bobbin.

TIP: *For consistently good stitches, remove thread and fabric lint that may collect under the throat plate and in the bobbin case area. Also oil the sites recommended in your sewing machine owner's manual.*

Sewing a Scant ¼" Seam

It's vital to the success of all your quiltmaking efforts—now and in the future—that you learn how to measure and accurately sew an exact scant ¼" seam.

Why a scant ¼" seam instead of a full ¼" seam? Using a scant sewn seam allowance (just one to two threads inside of a ¼" measurement) accommodates the seam allowance fold. In quiltmaking, both seam allowances are frequently pressed in one direction to help provide support to the stitches. The bulk created by two fabric layers pushed to one side can distort the accuracy of the ¼" seam.

Sewing an accurate scant ¼" seam allowance will be even easier with one of the following sewing-machine options:

- ¼" presser foot attachment

- ¼" seam allowance mark on the throat plate

- needle adjustment feature on the sewing machine

If your sewing machine lacks these features, check with the machine's manufacturer about the availability of a ¼" presser foot or a throat plate marked in ¼" segments. *Note:* While you're checking into availability for these attachments, you may also want to find out if a walking foot, and a darning or quilting foot are available. Later on in the quiltmaking process these feet are used when the quilt layers are stitched together.

throat plate with ¼" markings

Use a ¼" presser foot or the ¼" mark on the sewing machine's throat plate as an easy guide to sewing an accurate ¼" seam.

Marking Alternative

Without the option of a ¼" presser foot, a ¼" line on the throat plate, or the ability to change the sewing machine needle position, try this:

Use a strip of ¼"-gridded graph paper to locate the position. With your sewing machine needle unthreaded, insert the needle through the printed line. To mark the seam allowance position, place a piece of regular (or painter's blue) masking tape or a short stack of any size Post-it® notes on the sewing machine adjacent to the edge of the graph paper as shown at right.

For an alternate method, use a strip of ¼"-gridded graph paper to locate the ¼" seam allowance position. Mark it with a piece of painter's blue masking tape or a short stack of Post-it® notes placed adjacent to the graph paper.

Use a stack of Post-it® notes as an easy guide for sewing a ¼" seam.

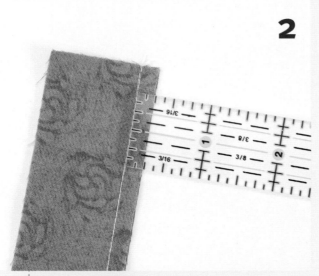

Measure the seam allowance for accuracy.

Testing a ¼" Seam

Test that the ¼" mark is accurate. To do this cut several small pieces of fabric that measure 1-½" x 3-½".

1. Thread your sewing machine. Place two pieces of fabric, right sides together with the long edges aligned. Following the guide, sew a scant ¼" seam along the 3-½" length as shown in Photo 1.

2. Measure the distance from the stitching to the raw edge of the fabric as shown in Photo 2. Correctly measured and sewn, the seam allowance should be slightly less than ¼".

what if:

If the test seam allowance does not measure a scant ¼", try sewing another seam. Adjust the note stack or masking tape, or alter how you feed the fabric into the machine. Test again.

3. When the first test seam allowance is accurate, with right sides together, sew a third piece of fabric to the second strip. As before, sew along the 3-½" length.

Press each seam allowance toward the darker fabric. The center strip should measure exactly 1". The three-strip set should measure exactly 3-½ x 3-½" as shown in Photo 3.

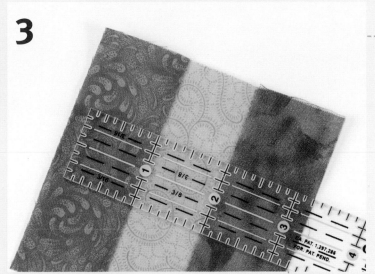

When all three test strips have been sewn together, press the seam allowances toward the dark fabric. The center strip should measure exactly 1".

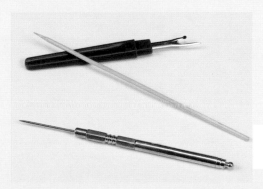

> **TIP:** *It's helpful to have a tool to guide fabric through the sewing machine, especially when you're working on a project where long sewn strips are needed. The handiest aid is a seam ripper. A bamboo skewer or a stiletto serve the same purpose.*

Moving Ahead

Now that you've learned to successfully sew accurate seams, you're ready to begin assembling the quilt top in each of the four simple quilt projects in Lesson Four.

lesson four

assembling the quilt top

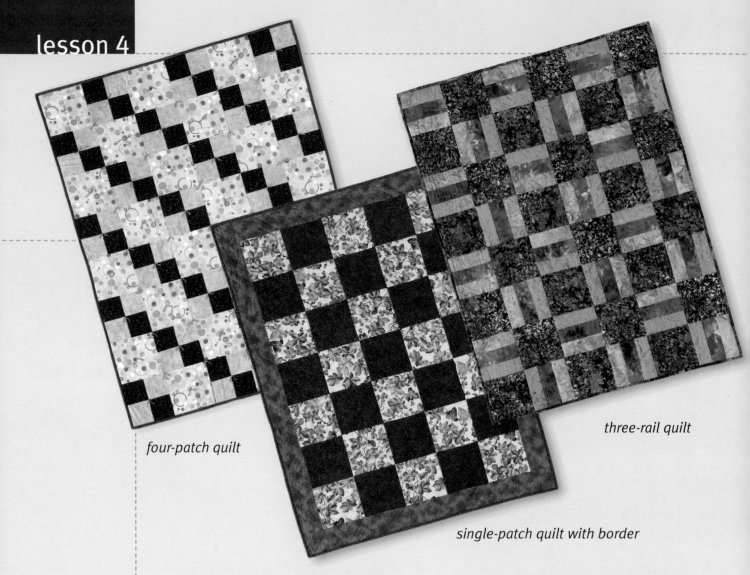

four-patch quilt

three-rail quilt

single-patch quilt with border

After you've gathered your tools and supplies, purchased and prepared the fabric, and practiced sewing accurate seams, the real fun begins. You're ready to assemble the quilt top.

For a quick start and fast finish, choose from three easy "tried and true" classic quilt patterns—four patch, single-patch, and three-rail—each sized just right for a 36 x 48" kid's quilt or wallhanging.

As a first-time quiltmaker, by starting small, in no time at all you'll have finished your first quilt!

Then use the techniques you've learned to take the three-in-one quilt challenge—a 42 x 54" quilt combining the three basic patterns complete with corner squares and inner and outer borders.

You'll find complete instructions for all four quilts on the following pages. Note, however, after you've assembled the quilt top for each project, we suggest you turn to Lessons Five and Six to learn about making the quilt sandwich and techniques for finishing the quilt prior to following the instructions for completing the quilt.

Designs for all four quilts were adapted from traditional block designs to a size that works up quickly for beginners by Linda Hungerford, project editor, while teaching first-time quiltmakers in Stitchin' Mission™ classes. (Turn to page 108 for an inspiring Gallery of quilts made by Stitchin' Mission™ first-time quiltmakers for charity.)

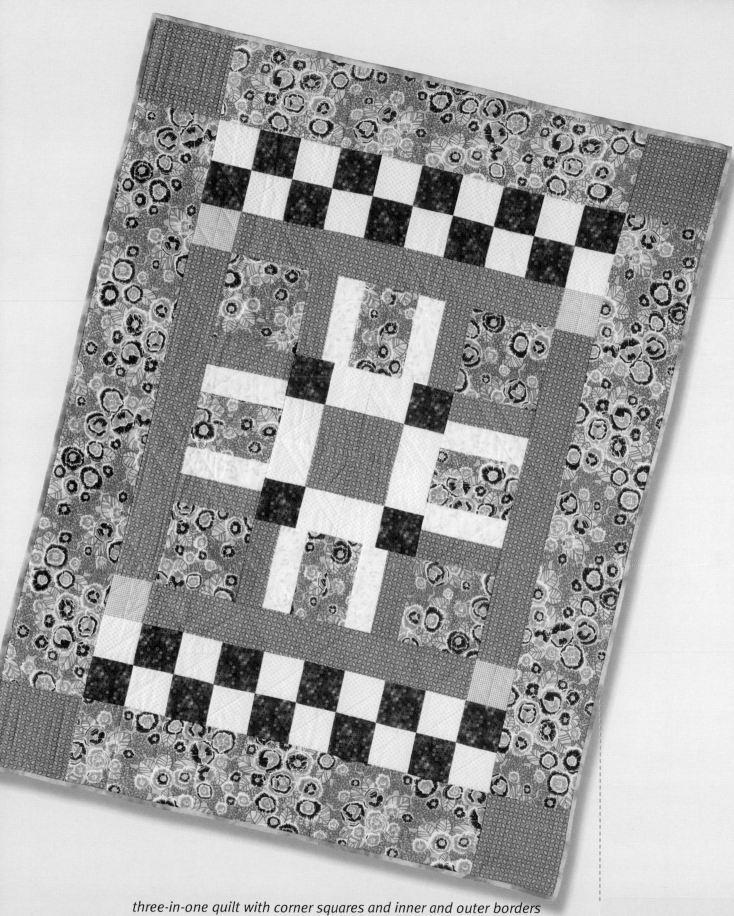

three-in-one quilt with corner squares and inner and outer borders

four-patch quilt

finished size with binding: 36-½ x 48-½"

Materials

- ¾ yard of pink print (focus fabric) for blocks

- ⅝ yard of lime green print for four-patch blocks

- ⅝ yard of purple print for four-patch blocks

- ⅓ yard of light purple print for binding

- 1-½ yards of coral print for backing

- 40 x 52" rectangle of quilt batting

- Sewing thread: neutral and to match binding

- Yarn or embroidery floss for ties

- Darning needle

Yardages are for 42/44"-wide, 100% cotton fabrics. All measurements include ¼" seam allowances. Sew with right sides together.

Cut the Fabric

Refer to Lesson Two, pages 24–31, for rotary-cutting techniques.

From pink print (focus fabric), cut:

- 4—6-½ x 42" strips, cut each strip into 6-½" squares for a total of 24 block squares

From lime green print, cut:

- 5—3-½ x 42" block strips

From purple print, cut:

- 5—3-½ x 42" block strips

From light purple print, cut:

- 5—2-¼ x 42" binding strips

From coral print, cut:

- 1—42 x 52" backing rectangle

four-patch quilt

Instructions

Assemble the Four-Patch Blocks

1. With right sides together, sew a purple block strip to a lime green block strip along the long edges as shown in Photo 1. Repeat to make a total of five strip sets. Press the seam allowances toward the purple strips. *Note:* Backstitching (the forward-backward machine stitching that secures stitches) is generally not needed when sewing quilts.

2. Referring to Lesson Two on page 26, straighten the left raw edge of each strip set as shown in Photo 2.

3. Cut a total of 48—3-½"-wide 2-square units from the strip sets as shown in Photo 3 and Diagram A. *Note:* Use a piece of masking tape to mark 3-½" on the ruler.

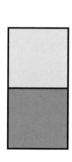

Diagram A

4. Align the raw edges of the 2-square units in pairs, with the seam allowances facing in opposite directions as shown in Photo 4. *Note:* This is called "nesting." When the pressed seam allowances are snugly joined together, corner seams are more likely to match.

four-patch quilt

5. Sew the first pair together along one long edge. *Note:* This is called "chain-piecing" or "chaining." Chain piece the remaining pairs together: do not cut the thread at the end of each pair. Continue sewing, guiding the next pair under the presser foot as shown in Photo 5 to make 24 four-patch blocks.

6. Cut the chain-pieced blocks apart as shown in Photo 6 and press the seam allowances one direction. *Note:* The seam allowance does not follow the "press toward the dark fabric" recommendation because the seam allowance falls across both medium and dark colors.

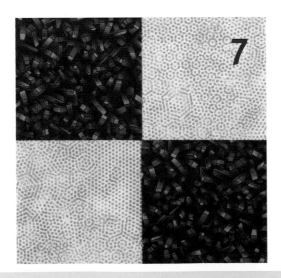

7. Your finished block as shown in Photo 7 should measure 6-½ x 6-½".

Assemble the Quilt Top

1. Lay out the 6-½" pink-print (focus fabric) block squares and four-patch blocks on a flat surface. Arrange the blocks using the Quilt Assembly Diagram on page 49 and the photo on page 42 as guides. It is important to arrange the blocks in eight rows with six blocks in each row to fit the backing.

2. Sew the blocks together in rows as shown in Diagram B. Press the seam allowances of Rows 1, 3, 5, and 7 to the left and the seam allowances of Rows 2, 4, 6, and 8 to the right.

3. Sew the rows together to complete the quilt top. Press the row seam allowances in one direction.

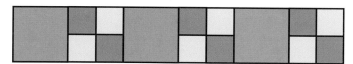

Rows 1, 3, 5 and 7

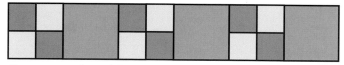

Rows 2, 4, 6 and 8

Diagram B

four-patch quilt

Complete the Quilt

Turn to Lesson Five (page 70) to learn about making the quilt sandwich and Lesson Six (page 88) for complete instructions on finishing the quilt before completing the quilt in the steps that follow.

1. Smooth out the backing rectangle on a flat surface with the wrong side up and center the batting on the backing. Center the quilt top, right side up, on top of the batting. Baste the layers together.

2. Place a tie at each block corner and at the center of each block. Thread needle with a long length of yarn; do not knot. Beginning in the center of the quilt, insert the needle through all layers at a corner of a block and return to the front about $\frac{1}{8}$" to $\frac{1}{4}$" away. Pull on the yarn to create a single strand 3" tail at the end.

3. Move to the next spot to be tied and take a small stitch through all layers. Continue across the quilt until a stitch is made at each planned tie location, rethreading the needle when needed. Clip the yarn between the stitches and tie a square knot at each point. Trim off excess yarn.

4. Sew the short ends of the 2-$\frac{1}{4}$"-wide light purple binding strips together with diagonal seams to form one long binding strip. Trim the seam allowances to $\frac{1}{4}$" and press open. Fold a 45-degree angle at the beginning of the binding; press. Fold the strip in half lengthwise with wrong sides together; press.

5. Beginning at the lower $\frac{1}{4}$ of the right edge, place the binding strip on the right side of the quilt, aligning the raw edges of the binding with the raw edges of the quilt top. *Note:* Follow the line you've drawn along the edge of the quilt top as recommended in Lesson Six on page 93. Pin the binding into place, as desired. Starting at the diagonal fold at the beginning edge of the binding, sew through all layers $\frac{1}{4}$" from the drawn line, mitering the corners. Pause stitching at the diagonal fold to cut away the excess binding, tucking the binding tail into the diagonal fold. Continue sewing to the beginning stitches. Trim the batting and backing $\frac{3}{8}$" from the stitching line. *Note:* Add a sleeve now, if desired.

6. Fold the binding to the back of the quilt to cover the machine stitching; press. Slip-stitch the folded edge of the binding to the back of the quilt.

7. Add a label, if desired.

Quilt Assembly Diagram

single-patch quilt

finished size with binding: 36-½ x 48-½"

Materials

- ⅝ yard of tan print (focus fabric) for blocks
- ⅝ yard of rust print for blocks
- ½ yard of green print for border
- ⅓ yard of dark green print for binding
- 1-½ yards of brown print for backing
- 40 x 52" rectangle of quilt batting
- Sewing thread: neutral and to match backing and binding
- Monofilament thread

Yardages are for 42/44"-wide, 100% cotton fabrics. All measurements include ¼" seam allowances. Sew with right sides together.

Cut the Fabric

Refer to Lesson Two, pages 24-31, for rotary-cutting techniques.

From tan print (focus fabric), cut:
- 3—6-½ x 42" strips, cut each strip into 6-½" squares for a total of 18 block squares

From rust print, cut:
- 3—6-½ x 42" strips, cut each strip into 6-½" squares for a total of 17 block squares

From green print, cut:
- 4—3-½ x 42" border strips

From dark green print, cut:
- 5—2-¼ x 42" binding strips

From brown print, cut:
- 1—42 x 52" backing rectangle

single-patch quilt

Instructions

Assemble the Quilt Center

1. Lay out the 6-½" tan (focus fabric) and rust print squares on a flat surface. Arrange the blocks as desired or use the Quilt Assembly Diagram on page 55 and the photo on page 50 as guides. It is important to arrange the blocks in seven rows with five blocks in each row to fit the backing and borders.

2. When you are pleased with the arrangement, sew the blocks together in rows as shown in Diagram A. Press the seam allowances of Rows 1, 3, 5, and 7 to the left and the seam allowances of Rows 2, 4, 6, and 8 to the right.

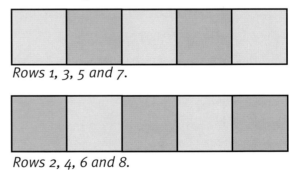

Rows 1, 3, 5 and 7.

Rows 2, 4, 6 and 8.

Diagram A

3. Sew the rows together as shown in Photo 1 to complete the quilt center as shown in Photo 2. Press the row seam allowances in one direction.

Assemble the Quilt Top

1. Measure the quilt length through the center as shown in Diagram B. Cut two green print border strips to this length. Sew the borders to the left and right edges of the quilt center. Press the seam allowances toward the borders.

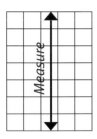

Measure

Diagram B

2. Measure the quilt width through the center including the borders as shown in Diagram C. Cut two green print border strips to this measurement. Sew the borders to the top and bottom edges of the quilt. Press the seam allowances toward the borders.

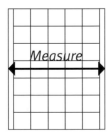

Measure

Diagram C

single-patch quilt

Complete the Quilt

Turn to Lesson Five (page 70) to learn about making the quilt sandwich and Lesson Six (page 88) for complete instructions on finishing the quilt before completing the quilt in the steps that follow.

1. Smooth out the backing rectangle on a flat surface with the wrong side up and center the batting on the backing. Center the quilt top, right side up, on top of the batting. Baste the layers together.

2. Thread your machine with monofilament thread in the top needle and thread to match the backing in the bobbin. Beginning in the center and working out to the edges, machine-quilt through all layers as desired or refer to Diagram D as a guide.

3. Sew the short ends of the 2 ¼"-wide dark green binding strips together with diagonal seams to form one long binding strip. Trim the seam allowances to ¼" and press open. Fold a 45-degree angle at the beginning of the binding; press. Fold the strip in half lengthwise with wrong sides together; press.

4. Beginning at the lower ¼ of the right edge, place the binding strip on the right side of the quilt, aligning the raw edges of the binding with the raw edges of the quilt top. *Note:* Follow the line you've drawn along the edge of the quilt top as recommended in Lesson Six on page 93. Pin the binding into place, as desired. Starting at the diagonal fold at the beginning edge of the binding, sew through all layers ¼" from the drawn line, mitering the corners. Pause stitching at the diagonal fold to cut away the excess binding, tucking the binding tail into the diagonal fold. Continue sewing to the beginning stitches. Trim the batting and backing ⅜" from the stitching line. *Note:* Add a sleeve now, if desired.

5. Fold the binding to the back of the quilt to cover the machine stitching; press. Slip-stitch the folded edge of the binding to the back of the quilt.

6. Add a label, if desired.

Diagram D

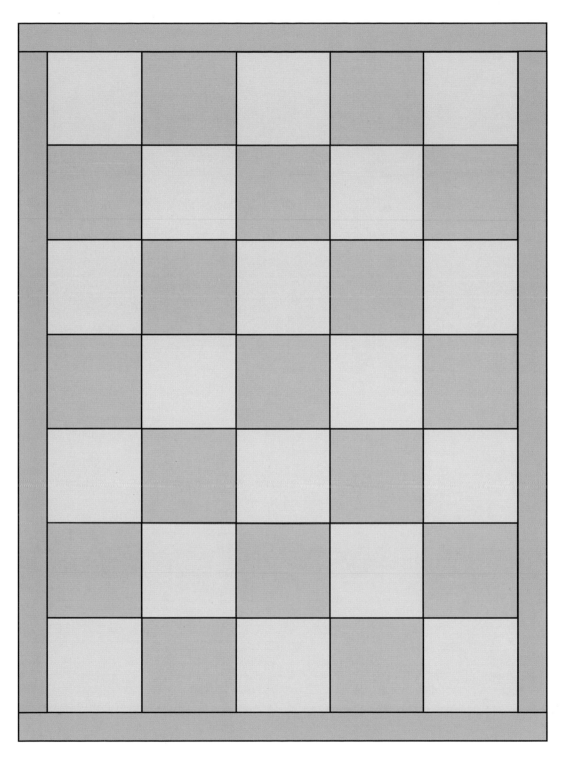

Quilt Assembly Diagram

three-rail quilt

finished size with binding: 36-½ x 48-½"

Materials

- ¾ yard of dark green print (focus fabric) for blocks

- ⅓ yard of green print for three-rail blocks

- ⅓ yard of blue print for three-rail blocks

- ⅓ yard of peach print for three-rail blocks

- ⅓ yard of green/pink print for binding

- 1-½ yards of light green print for backing

- 40 x 52" rectangle of quilt batting

- Sewing thread: neutral and to match backing and binding

- Monofilament thread

Yardages are for 42/44"-wide, 100% cotton fabrics. All measurements include ¼" seam allowances. Sew with right sides together.

Cut the Fabric

Refer to Lesson Two, pages 24–31, for rotary-cutting techniques.

From dark green print (focus fabric), cut:

- 4—6-½ x 42" strips, cut each strip into 6-½" squares for a total of 24 block squares

From green print, cut:

- 4—2-½ x 42" block strips

From blue print, cut:

- 4—2-½ x 42" block strips

From peach print, cut:

- 4—2-½ x 42" block strips

From green/pink print cut:

- 5—2-¼ x 42" binding strips

From light green, cut:

- 1—42 x 52" backing rectangle

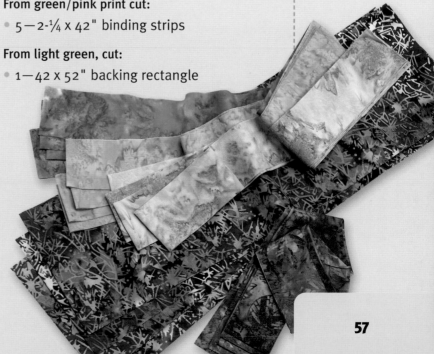

three-rail quilt

Instructions

Assemble the Three-Rail Blocks

1. With right sides together, sew a 2-½"-wide green block strip to a 2-½"-wide blue block strip along the long edges as shown in Photo 1.

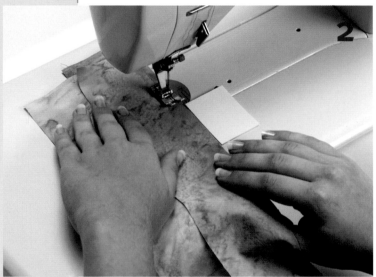

2. Sew a 2-½"-wide peach block strip to the remaining long edge of the blue block strip as shown in Photo 2 to complete one strip set. Repeat Steps 1 and 2 to make a total of four strips sets. Press the seam allowances toward the darker fabric.

3. Referring to Lesson Two on page 26, straighten the left raw edges of each strip set as shown in Photo 3.

4. Cut a total of 24—6-½"-wide units from the strip sets as shown in Photo 4.

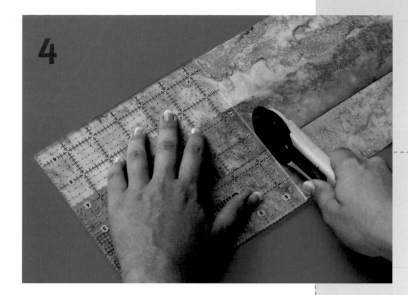

5. Your finished block as shown in Photo 5 should measure 6-½ x 6-½".

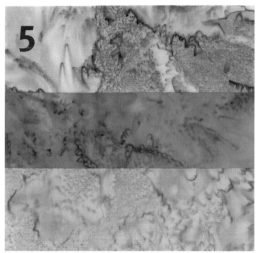

Assemble the Quilt Top

1. Lay out the 6-½" dark green-print (focus fabric) block squares and three-rail blocks on a flat surface. Arrange the blocks as desired or use the Quilt Assembly Diagram on page 61 and the photo on page 56 as guides. It is important to arrange the blocks in eight rows with six blocks in each row to fit the backing.

2. Sew the blocks together in rows as shown in Diagram A, being careful to maintain the direction of the three-rail blocks for correct color placement. Press the seam allowances of Rows 1, 3, 5, and 7 to the left and the seam allowances of Rows 2, 4, 6, and 8 to the right.

3. Sew the rows together to complete the quilt top. Press the row seam allowances in one direction.

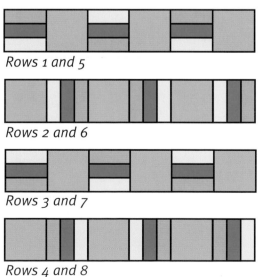

Rows 1 and 5

Rows 2 and 6

Rows 3 and 7

Rows 4 and 8

Diagram A

three-rail quilt

Complete the Quilt

Turn to Lesson Five (page 70) to learn about making the quilt sandwich and Lesson Six (page 88) for complete instructions on finishing the quilt before completing the quilt in the steps that follow.

1. Smooth the backing rectangle on a flat surface with the wrong side up and center the batting on the backing. Center the quilt top, right side up, on top of the batting. Baste the layers together.

2. Thread your machine with monofilament thread in the top needle and thread to match the backing in the bobbin. Beginning in the center and working out to the edges, machine-quilt through all layers as desired or refer to Diagram B as a guide.

3. Sew the short ends of the 2-¼"-wide green/pink binding strips together with diagonal seams to form one long binding strip. Trim the seam allowances to ¼" and press open. Fold a 45-degree angle at the beginning of the binding; press. Fold the strip in half lengthwise with wrong sides together; press.

4. Beginning at the lower ¼ of the right edge, place the binding strip on the right side of the quilt, aligning the raw edges of the binding with the raw edges of the quilt top. *Note:* Follow the line you've drawn along the edge of the quilt top as recommended in Lesson Six on page 93. Pin the binding into place, as desired. Starting at the diagonal fold at the beginning edge of the binding, sew through all layers ¼" from the drawn line, mitering the corners. Pause stitching at the diagonal fold to cut away the excess binding, tucking the binding tail into the diagonal fold. Continue sewing to the beginning stitches. Trim the batting and backing ⅜" from the stitching line.
Note: Add a sleeve now, if desired.

5. Fold the binding to the back of the quilt to cover the machine stitching. Slip-stitch the folded edge of the binding to the back of the quilt.

6. Add a label, if desired.

Diagram B

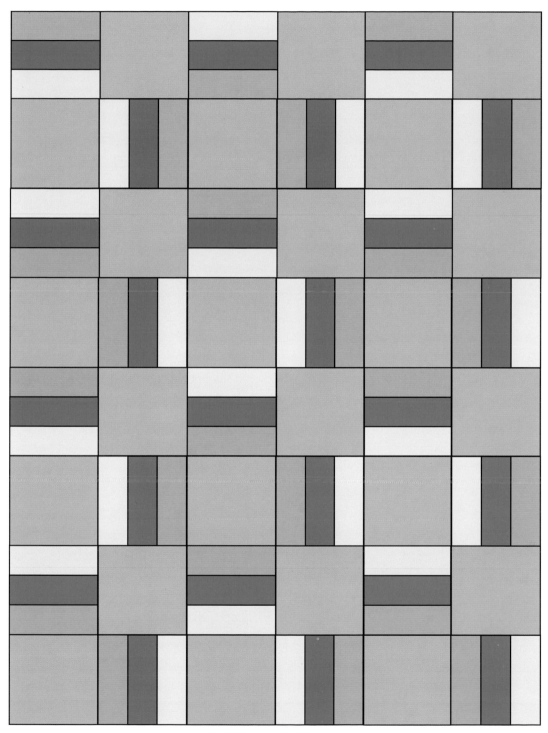

Quilt Assembly Diagram

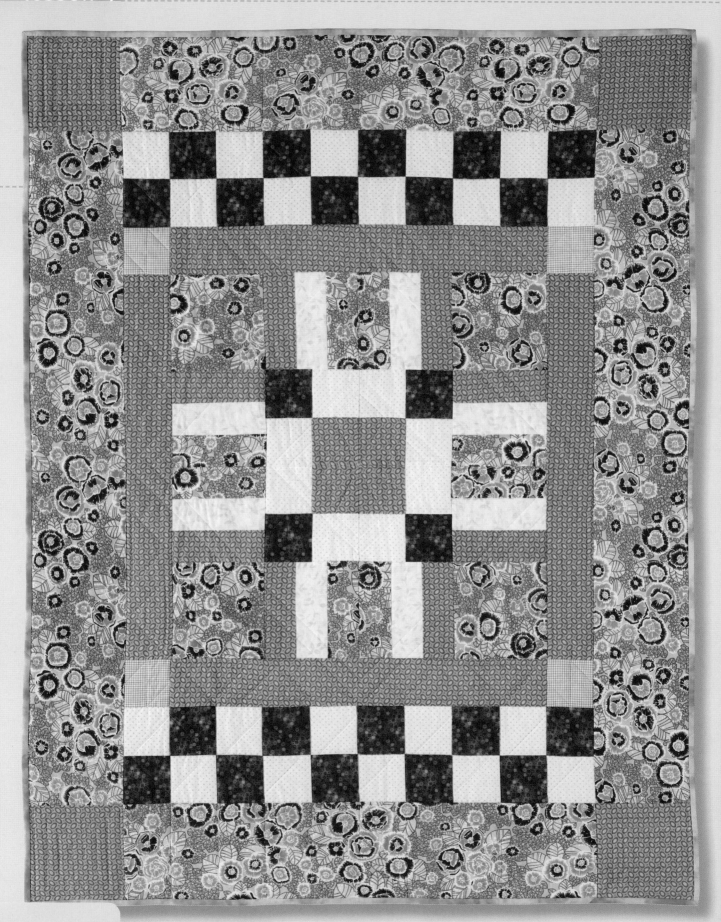

three-in-one quilt

finished size with binding: 42-½ x 54-½"

Materials

- 1-¼ yards of green print (focus fabric) for blocks and outer border

- 1 yard of blue print for three-rail blocks, inner border, and outer corner squares

- ⅓ yard of dark pink print for four-patch blocks

- ½ yard of white print for four-patch blocks

- ½ yard of blue for binding

- ¼ yard of pale pink print for three-rail blocks

- 1 fat quarter pink-and-white check for inner cornerstones

- 3-⅝ yards of coordinating fabric for backing

- 46 x 58" rectangle of quilt batting

- Sewing thread: neutral and to match backing and binding

- Monofilament thread

Yardages are for 42/44"-wide, 100% cotton fabrics. All measurements include ¼" seam allowances. Sew with right sides together.

Cut the Fabric

Refer to Lesson Two, pages 24–31, for rotary-cutting techniques.

From green print (focus fabric), cut:

- 5—6-½ x 42" strips, cut 4—6-½" block squares and reserve remaining strips for outer border

- 2—2-½ x 42" block strips

From blue print, cut:

- 1—6-½ x 42" strip, cut 4—6-½" corner squares

- 4—3-½ x 42" strips, cut 4—3-½" four-patch squares and reserve remaining strips for inner border

- 2—2-½ x 42" block strips

From dark pink print, cut:

- 3—3-½ x 42" block strips

From white print, cut:

- 3—3-½ x 42" strips, cut 4—3-½" four-patch squares and reserve remaining strips for block strips

- 2—2-½ x 42" block strips

From blue, cut:

- 6—2-½ x 42" binding strips

From pale pink print, cut:

- 2—2-½ x 42" block strips

From pink-and-white check, cut:

- 4—3-½" cornerstones

From coordinating fabric, cut:

- 1—42 x 58" backing rectangle

- 2—2-½ x 58" backing rectangles

three-in-one quilt

Instructions

Assemble the Two-Color Four-Patch Blocks

1. With right sides together, sew a 3-½"-wide dark pink print strip to a 3-½"-wide white print strip along the long edges for one strip set. Repeat to make a total of three strip sets. Press the seam allowances toward the darker fabric.

2. Referring to Lesson Two on page 26, straighten the left raw edge of each strip set. Cut a total of 24—3-½" wide 2-square units from the strip sets as shown in Diagram A. Set aside 4 of the 2-square units for the three-color four-patch blocks in the center of the quilt.

Diagram A

3. Sew 20 of the 2-square units together in pairs as shown in Diagram B. Press the seam allowances one direction. Your finished block should measure 6-½ x 6-½".

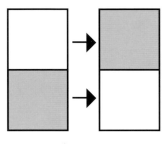

Diagram B

Assemble the Three-Color Four-Patch Blocks

1. Sew together the 3-½" blue print and white print squares in pairs as shown in Diagram C to make four 2-square units.

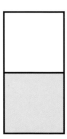

Diagram C

2. Sew together the 2-square units in pairs, using one blue and white unit with each dark pink and white unit as shown in Diagram D. Press the seam allowances one direction. Your finished block should measure 6-½ x 6-½".

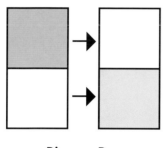

Diagram D

Assemble the Three-Rail Blocks

1. With right sides together, sew a 2-½"-wide green print strip (focus fabric) to a 2-½"-wide pale pink print strip along the long edges.

2. Sew a 2-½"-wide blue print strip to the remaining long edge of the pale pink strip to complete the strip set. Repeat Steps 1 and 2 to make a second strip set. Press the seam allowances toward the darker fabrics.

3. Referring to Lesson Two on page 26 straighten the left raw edge of each strip set. Cut a total of 8—6-½"-wide units from the strip sets. Your finished block as shown in Diagram E should measure 6-½ x 6-½".

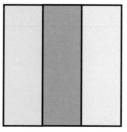

Diagram E

three-in-one quilt

Assemble the Quilt Center

1. Lay out the 4—6-½" green print block squares, 8 three-rail blocks, and 4 three-color four-patch blocks on a flat surface, using Diagram F as a guide.

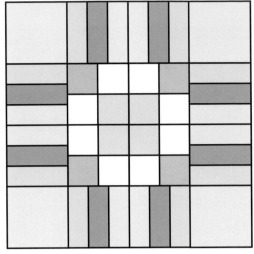

Diagram F

2. Sew the blocks together in rows as shown in Diagram G, being careful to maintain the direction of the pieced blocks for correct color placement. Press the seam allowances of Rows 1 and 3 to the left and the seam allowances of Rows 2 and 4 to the right.

Rows 1 and 4

Rows 2 and 3

Diagram G

3. Sew the rows together to complete the quilt center. Press the row seam allowances one direction.

Assemble the Quilt Top

1. Measure the quilt length as shown in Diagram H. Cut two 3-½"-wide blue print inner border strips to this length.

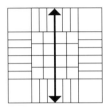

Diagram H

2. Measure the quilt width as shown in Diagram I. Cut two 3-½"-wide blue print inner border strips to this length.

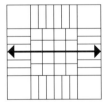

Diagram I

3. Sew the borders from Step 1 to the left and right edges of the quilt center. Press the seam allowances toward the borders.

Diagram J

4. Sew a 3-½" pink-and-white check cornerstone to each end of each border from Step 2 as shown in Diagram J. Press the seam allowances toward the borders.

5. Sew the pieced borders to the top and bottom edges of the quilt center. Press the seam allowances toward the borders.

6. Sew together the two-color four-patch blocks to make two rows of 5 blocks as shown in Diagram K. Press all seam allowances the same direction. Sew the block rows to the top and bottom edges of the quilt.

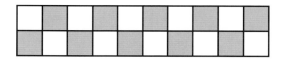

Diagram K

7. Measure the quilt length through the center and cut two 6-½"-wide green print (focus fabric) outer border strips to this length.

8. Measure the quilt width through the center and cut two 6-½"-wide green print (focus fabric) outer border strips to this length.

9. Sew the borders from Step 7 to the left and right edges of the quilt. Press the seam allowances toward the borders.

10. Sew a 6-½" blue print corner square to each end of each border from Step 8. Press the seam allowances toward the borders.

11. Sew the pieced borders to the top and bottom edges of the quilt. Press the seam allowances toward the borders.

Assemble the Backing

1. To piece the quilt backing, sew together the long edges of the backing rectangles as shown in Diagram L, with a ½" seam allowance. Press the seam allowances away from the center.

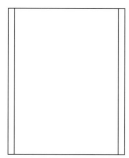

Diagram L

three-in-one quilt

Complete the Quilt

Turn to Lesson Five (page 70) to learn about making the quilt sandwich and Lesson Six (page 88) for complete instructions on finishing the quilt before completing the quilt in the steps that follow.

1. Smooth out the backing on a flat surface with the wrong side up and center the batting on the backing. Center the quilt top, right side up, on top of the batting. Baste the layers together.

3. Thread your machine with monofilament thread in the top needle and thread to match the backing in the bobbin. Beginning in the center and working out to the edges, machine-quilt through all layers as desired or refer to Diagram M as a guide.

4. Sew the short ends of the 2-¼"-wide blue binding strips together with diagonal seams to form one long binding strip. Trim the seam allowances to ¼" and press open. Fold a 45-degree angle at the beginning of the binding; press. Fold the strip in half lengthwise with wrong sides together; press.

5. Beginning at the lower ¼ of the right edge, place the binding strip on the right side of the quilt, aligning the raw edges of the binding with the raw edges of the quilt top. *Note:* Follow the line you've drawn along the edge of the quilt top as recommended in Lesson Six on page 93. Pin the binding into place, as desired. Starting at the diagonal fold at the beginning edge of the binding, sew through all layers ¼" from the drawn line, mitering the corners. Pause stitching at the diagonal fold to cut away the excess binding, tucking the binding tail into the diagonal fold. Continue sewing to the beginning stitches. Trim the batting and backing ⅜" from the stitching line. *Note:* Add a sleeve now, if desired.

6. Fold the binding to the back of the quilt to cover the machine stitching. Slip-stitch the folded edge of the binding to the back of the quilt.

7. Add a label, if desired.

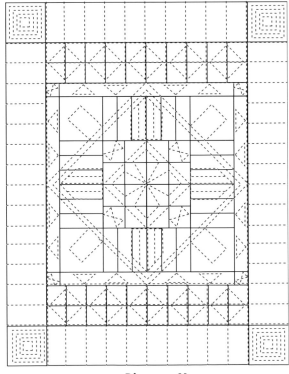

Diagram M

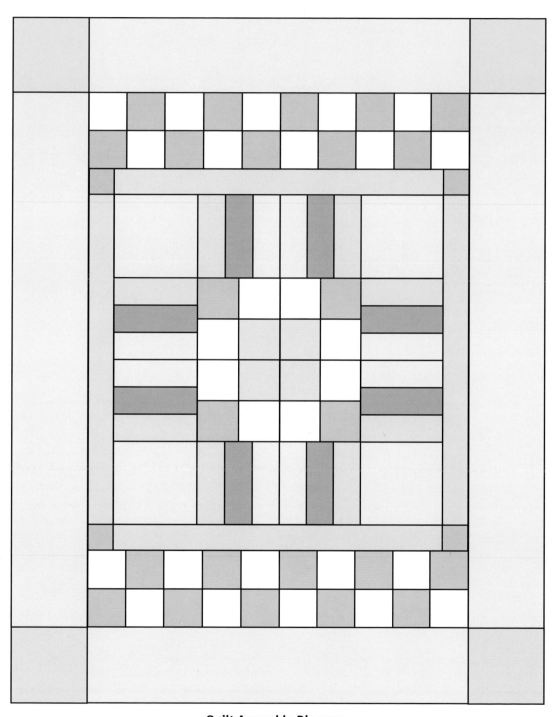

Quilt Assembly Diagram

lesson five
making the quilt sandwich

what you need to know about batting

When you're ready to layer and baste because you have completed a quilt top, you'll need a quilt batt and backing fabric to make a quilt sandwich. Batting choices are nearly as varied as fabric choices. Several manufacturers have developed battings made from polyester and cotton, and blends of both. You can even find wool, silk, cashmere, and alpaca in batting. As with every decision, several factors play into choosing the batting that's right for your quilt.

polyester batting if you prefer a puffier look. The ¼" polyester thickness can be tied together. *Note:* In Lesson Six you'll learn how to tie a quilt with regularly-placed knots that permanently hold the quilt sandwich together.

Choose a low-loft batting if you prefer a flatter appearance. Low loft cotton batting moves well beneath your sewing machine pressure foot if you decide to quilt by machine. *Note:* In Lesson Six you'll learn about machine quilting.

Loft

Loft is the height or thickness of the batting. The denseness of fibers contribute to the batting's loftiness. As a general rule, choose a ¼" loft

> **TIP:** *Batting is available in several neutral shades—white, cream, charcoal gray, and black. Choose the shade that blends best with your fabric colors.*

A wide variety of battings are available in cotton, polyester, or a blend of both. Battings shown are from left to right: Quilter's Dream® Request; Fairfield® Soft Touch; Warm & White; Hobb's®; Quilter's Dream; and Mountain Mist®.

Read a batting's packaging information. It can tell you a lot about what it is, how it handles, and how to care for it.

Reading the Label

Read the quilt batting label for information about its suitability for tying or quilting by machine. Batting for tying should indicate that it's okay to place ties 3" to 4" apart. Some battings permit ties or stitches from 6" to 12" apart. If you're uncertain, ask your fabric shop clerk for a recommendation. As with fabric, expect to invest a little more money in a higher quality product.

Cutting the Batting

For the quilt sandwich, the batting that is usually cut using a measurement that is several inches larger than the quilt top to allow for "wiggle room" for centering the quilt top. For example, a 36 x 48" quilt top would require a piece of batting that is 40 x 52".

Note: Excess batting and backing fabric will be trimmed away before the binding is added.

TIP: *If you purchase batting that has been packaged in a tight roll, let it "air" before layering it in a quilt sandwich. To restore the loft, unwrap the batting and either allow it to lay out for several hours or briefly tumble it in the dryer on the air fluff setting.*

what you need to know about the quilt backing

When choosing a quilt back, select a fabric of similar quality to the fabrics used in the quilt top. The washability and durability of a finished quilt is most consistent when the fabrics on the front are compatible with the fabric on the back. Avoid using a bed sheet for a quilt back. A sheet may include polyester or rayon, making it incompatible with a quilt top. Also, a sheet may be made with fabric that has a higher thread count than quilting cotton, making it difficult to tie or quilt by hand or machine.

Cutting the Backing

The backing size is determined in the same way as the batting size. Use a measurement that is several inches larger than the quilt top to allow "wiggle room" for centering the quilt top. For three of the featured quilts you'll be able to use a single, whole piece of fabric. For example, 36 x 48" quilt top requires a backing that is 42 x 52".

Note: Excess batting and backing fabric will be trimmed away before the binding is added.

For the three-in-one quilt featured on page 62, strips of fabric are added to the backing fabric to accommodate the width of the quilt top.

Removing Selvages

Because selvages can cause distortion or puckering, remove the selvages from each of the two pieces. Join the pieces together along the cut selvage edges, using a ½" seam for greater durability.

what if:

If you need a quilt back that's more than 42" in width, simply sew together several pieces of fabric to make a backing that's large enough to accommodate the quilt top.

Be Creative

For an interesting quilt back, piece together scraps of fabric from the quilt top, or any other fabrics that coordinate with the quilt top. The possibilities are as varied as your imagination. Pieced quilt backs are also called "back art."

Pieced backs not only add to a quilt's character, but are an economical way to use the fabric you already have on hand. When the quilt back is as attractive as the quilt top, it can be reversed for double-duty.

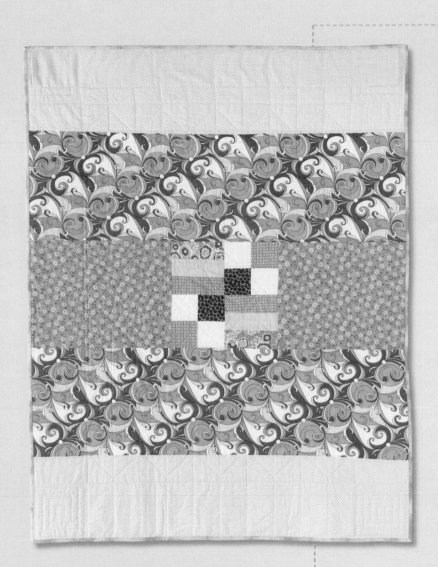

Let your imagination be your guide to creating a scrap-happy quilt back.

what you need to know about layering the quilt sandwich

When you've settled on a batting and prepared a backing, you're ready to make your quilt sandwich.

Work Surface

Choose a hard surface upon which to layer the pieces. A table is preferable because the height may cause less back strain, but sometimes the only option for sandwiching a large quilt is the floor. Avoid carpeting though, as the pile doesn't allow the quilt to lay flat.

what if:

If you don't have a table that's large enough, ask a nearby community center, church, or quilt shop if it's possible to schedule a time when you can go in, push tables together, and baste. Invite one or more friends to join you, not only to accomplish the task more quickly, but to enjoy time together. Just remember that you may be asked to return the favor!

TIP: *You may choose to make your quilt sandwich on the floor. If your hardwood, tile, or laminate flooring is patterned with lines or geometrics, utilize the design to square the backing, thereby also squarely layering the batting and quilt top.*

You'll Need

- A hard surface work area, preferably at least as large as the quilt backing
- TOP LAYER—the pressed quilt top with all seams laying flat
- FILLER LAYER—the batting that measures several inches larger than the quilt top
- BOTTOM LAYER—the cut and pressed backing fabric that measures several inches larger than the quilt top
- A roll of masking tape

Before you start building your "sandwich," be sure the backing fabric has been well-pressed so it will lay flat. Then, with the wrong side facing up, lay the backing on the work surface. Smooth the fabric from the center outward. Avoid pulling the fabric too taut.

1. Place a piece of masking tape near the middle of one edge of the quilt backing. Repeat for the opposite side. Complete taping on these two sides as shown in Photo 1. Repeat the process on the remaining two sides, taping every few inches to secure the backing to the work surface.

Push tables together to accommodate the quilt back and use masking tape to secure the backing to the table.

2. To center the batting on top of the quilt backing, fold the batting into fourths and place the center fold point over the center of the backing, smoothing it from the center outward as shown in Photo 2.

Position the batting on the wrong side of the backing fabric. Taping is not necessary because the batting "sticks" to the backing.

3. Position the quilt top (right side up) on the batting as shown in Photo 3, following the same process to center and smooth it as you did with the batting. After the quilt top is positioned on the batting, be sure that the quilt top is within the edges of the batting and backing. Check this—and then recheck this— before you begin to pin-baste the layers together.

When you're making a large quilt, to center the quilt top on the batting, fold the top into fourths. Then position the corner of the folded edges in the center of the batting.

what you need to know about basting the quilt sandwich

As a first-time quiltmaker, you have two basting options. Our recommended method uses 1" to 1-½" (size 1 or size 2) nickel-plated safety pins. The other method uses items you probably already have—a needle and thread. Both have the same result: holding the layers together until the quilt sandwich is tied or quilted.

Use safety pins when you expect to complete quilting quickly by machine quilting or tying. Use needle and thread basting when you expect to hand quilt—a quilting process that takes more time. *Note:* Over a long period of time, safety pins left in a quilt top may leave permanent marks or small holes on the quilt.

You'll Need

- 1" to 1-½" (size 1 or size 2) nickel-plated safety pins
- A tool for closing the safety pins such as a grapefruit spoon or a purchased Kwik Klip™

TIP: *Buy nickel-plated safety pins. The coating on the safety pins gives an added measure of protection. If you leave the pins in the fabric longer than you intended, rust marks may be less likely to appear later.*

Basting with Safety Pins

Open 1" to 1 ½" safety pins and scatter them across the quilt top. Pick up a pin with your dominant hand and insert it into the quilt top, through all layers of the quilt sandwich. Place safety pins approximately four to five inches apart. Close the safety pin with both hands, or use a grapefruit spoon or a Kwik Klip™.

TIP: *Use a key, a grapefruit spoon, or a purchased safety pin closer to easily close safety pins. If you're right-handed, hold the closer in your left hand. While holding the safety pin with your right-hand, place the closer beneath the pin tip and guide it into the safety pin head.*

The Kwik Klip™ is held in the left hand and used to lift the safety pin tip to the safety pin head.

Passing the Fist Test

An easy test to know whether you have basted with enough safety pins is to place your fist anywhere on the quilt top. A safety pin should be very close, or touching your fist.

It saves time if you decide in advance what quilting pattern or tying layout you'll follow and avoid placing safety pins in those locations.

When two people are working together, the quiltmaker should insert the safety pins while the "helper" closes the safety pins. The quiltmaker should place the safety pins according to a pre-selected tying or machine quilting pattern.

Note: Using straight pins to baste a quilt should be avoided because of the likelihood of a pricked finger which will be painful as well as possibly cause staining of the quilt.

Give your pin-basted quilt the fist test. A safety pin should be very close to, or touching your fist.

what if:

If after basting the quilt sandwich you realize that you did not center the quilt top within the edges of the quilt backing and quilt batting, remove the basting pins and reposition the quilt top.

what you need to know about quilting the sandwich

As a first-time quilter choose a simple design to hold the layers together for machine quilting. Begin with straight stitching, at least until you're comfortable guiding all the layers beneath the presser foot. This method requires no marking. Just stitch along the seam lines as closely as possible.

When stitching-in-the-ditch, sew along the seam. Guide the quilt on the "downside"— the side without the seam allowance underneath—to avoid stitching "bobbles."

Stitch-in-the-Ditch Quiltiing

Many quilters find it's easiest to routinely use the stitch-in-the-ditch method for machine quilting. It's a great beginning for stabilizing a quilt before adding other quilting designs.

FREE MOTION QUILTING

If you're interested in free-motion quilting which combines lowering or covering the feed dogs (teeth under the sewing machine needle) and using both hands to guide the quilt sandwich—take some time to first learn more about it. For first-time quiltmakers, free-motion quilting may be daunting. Plan to learn more from a reliable machine quilting instructor.

HAND QUILTING

If you want to hand quilt, keep in mind that it is satisfying but time-consuming. Many first-time quiltmakers are looking for the quick reward of accomplishment, and admittedly, hand quilting takes more time. Plan to learn more from a reliable hand quilting instructor.

Grid Quilting

Mark a simple grid design on the quilt surface. Align a long rotary ruler diagonally with the intersections of blocks. Then, use a piece of chalk, water-erasable marker, or a sliver of soap to lightly draw quilting lines.

Straight-line quilting on a single-patch block, in a simple grid design, adds interest and dimension to a quilt.

Echo Quilting

Follow and repeat the shape of a block. Just as a stone tossed into a pool of water creates ripples, so does echo quilting as it repeats the design.

As you gain confidence in machine quilting, experiment with a combination of stitch-in-the-ditch, grid quilting, and echo quilting for a one-of-a-kind quilted masterpiece.

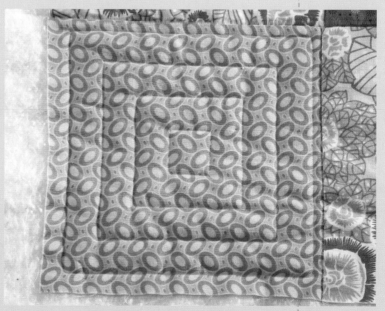

An example of echo-quilting, in which a shape is repeated.

On the left, monofilament thread, also known as "invisible thread," is shown in clear and smoke. On the right are several cotton threads in varying weights: 50-weight two-ply and three-ply, and 40- and 28-weights.

Choosing Thread

Nylon monofilament thread is good for first-time machine quilters. With monofilament, inexperienced quilters can make nearly invisible quilting stitches. Not surprisingly, monofilament is also known as "invisible thread." It's available in clear and smoke, but choose smoke only if your fabric colors are mostly dark. Thread your sewing machine with the monofilament on top.

For the bobbin, choose a thread color that closely matches the quilt backing. This is so the stitches will blend into the backing. As a bonus, any bobbles you might make won't show.

Lengthening the Stitch

For thread, the higher the number, the finer the thread. For example, 60-weight thread is finer than 50-weight thread. For 50-weight thread use a size 75/11 quilting needle or size 70/10 jeans needle. For thread that's 40-weight or heavier, choose a size 90/14 quilting needle or a size 80/12 or 90/14 jeans needle.When you begin a line of quilting, take several stitches in the same place, then gradually lengthen the stitch, taking several stitches very close together before lengthening the stitch to 8 to 10 stitches per inch. Use these stitches at the beginning and end of quilting to help secure the threads.

When using monofilament thread, it's a good idea to test it in your sewing machine. With nylon monofilament thread threaded through the top, and cotton thread on the bottom, you may find that your sewing machine tension—the balance between the top thread and bottom thread—needs to be adjusted.

TIP: *Beginner machine quilters should avoid thread labeled "quilting thread." Though it's possible to machine quilt with quilting thread, it's intended for hand-quilting and any machine-use should be attempted by experienced machine quilters.*

Adjusting the Tension

To adjust your machine's tension control, change to a higher number for more tension on the top thread, or change to a lower number to loosen the tension on the top thread.

To make sure the tension is adjusted correctly, make a mini-"test quilt." Cut and layer 6" squares of fabric and batting. Machine-quilt these squares to check the tension and the stitch length before beginning to quilt your project.

If your machine doesn't handle the monofilament, try machine quilting with cotton thread on the top as well as in the bobbin. Keep in mind that the stitches will be more visible.

TIP: *A sliver of bar soap is a readily-available marking "tool."*

Transferring the Design

If you'd like to draw a quilting design on your quilt before you begin to stitch, use one of several commercial marking tools, choosing light or dark that contrasts with the colors of your quilt. Consider which markers can be brushed off the quilt top, or may need to be washed out when the quilting is finished. *Note:* Lead pencils may leave markings that may not wash out.

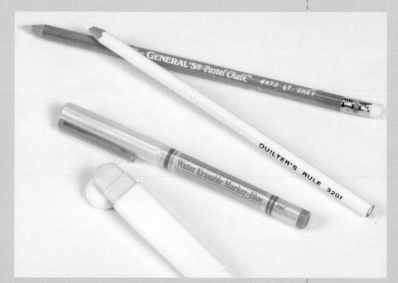

Depending on the colors in your quilt top, use one of these notions to mark your quilting design: (top to bottom) marking pencils in gray or white, a blue water erasable marker, a chalk-o-liner.

what you need to know about machine quilting

Machine quilting is a quick and attractive way to quilt. For your first attempt, try machine quilting using only straight lines. You'll also gain more experience guiding the quilt sandwich under the presser foot. Quilting stitches (versus tying) by machine or by hand also highlight and enhance the piecework of your quilt.

Setting Up the Machine

Before setting up your sewing machine for quilting, make sure it's clean. Remove the latest build-up of lint from under the throat plate and in the bobbin area. The machine should be oiled and "happily purring."

Any of these sewing machine feet can be used for machine quilting. The "walking feet" on the left are for even-feeding multiple layers of fabric. The two feet on the right are darning feet—one is open-toed to make it easier to see where you're stitching.

Choosing a Walking Foot

If you've been using a ¼" presser foot, change to the standard sewing machine foot. Or, if your sewing machine has a walking foot, attach to use for straight-line machine quilting. The rubber grippers on the bottom of the walking foot work in conjunction with the sewing machine's feed dogs (teeth under the needle) to move both the top fabric and the bottom fabric through the sewing machine at the same rate. A walking foot is especially helpful when sewing through the thickness of multiple layers. A variety of walking feet options are described in the photo on the left.

Changing the Needle

Change the sewing machine needle from the one used for assembling the quilt top to one that's thicker and stronger for quilting through the three sandwich layers.

A size 75/11 quilting needle or a size 80/12 jeans needle may be best, however the needle size also depends on the size of the thread you're using, and the thickness of the quilt sandwich. *Note:* For needles, the higher the number, the larger the needle. For example: a size 90/14 needle is larger than a size 80/12 needle.

For machine quilting, change your sewing machine needle to one that's thicker and stronger for stitching through multiple layers of fabric.

Removing Safety Pins

If you've safety-pin basted your quilt sandwich, you'll find it's easy to remove the pins as you quilt. Just don't attempt to sew over safety pins; you and your sewing machine needle will lose.

what you need to know about tying the quilt

Tying a quilt is faster than machine quilting, and it's a perfectly acceptable way to finish your first—or second or third!—quilt. Tied quilts are durable and easily washed, making them great for babies and small children, or to use as a picnic cloth. Choose either yarn or heavy thread for tying quilt layers together. Yarn choices include polyester, rayon, wool, and cotton fibers. Thread choices include embroidery floss and pearl cotton. Yarn is easy to work with and appears more pronounced on the quilt surface. As always when working with colors of fabric, yarn, or thread,

exercise caution with the colors red and dark blue. If you're in doubt, don't use those yarn or thread colors, or test for colorfastness following the instructions on page 23.

You'll need a sturdy, large-eyed needle. Choose a darning needle, size 14 to 18. The eye size will be large enough for the thickness of yarn or heavy thread, and the sharp point will pierce the layers of fabric and batting.

Tying the Quilt

Tying is accomplished in a manner similar to thread-basting. Cut a length of yarn that is slightly longer than your quilt, from one end to another. Thread one strand through your darning needle. Without knotting, and beginning at the center of the basted quilt sandwich, take an up-down stitch, approximately ⅛" to ¼" wide through all three layers.

Keep the yarn in one piece, taking a stitch at regular intervals.

1. Keep the yarn in one piece, taking a stitch at regular intervals according to the tying layout as shown in Photo 1.

> **TIP:** *If you're concerned about a knot coming untied, perhaps because the yarn or thread is somewhat slippery, take a second stitch through all the layers, before tying the knot. Take stitches at the intersection of pieced blocks to hide any block intersections that don't match.*

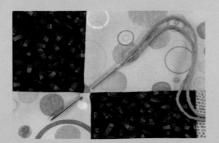

2. Snip the yarn between each stitch as shown in Photo 2.

3. Tie the cut ends together, making a square knot—right over left, left over right, referring to the chart below.

Snip the yarn between each stitch.

HOW TO TIE A SQUARE KNOT

With a single strand of yarn, take a ⅛" to ¼" stitch through all three layers. Make a square knot–right over left; left over right.

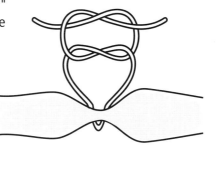

top →

batting →

backing →

4. Trim all ties to a consistent length, approximately ½" to 1" as shown in Photo 4.

Trim all ties to a consistent length.

lesson
six
finishing the quilt

what you need to know about binding

Finish your quilt by machine sewing a continuous strip of binding around all four edges of your quilt sandwich to cover the raw fabric edges. There are numerous techniques for binding a quilt, but double-fold binding is the most durable because, as the name implies, the raw edges of the quilt are wrapped with two layers of fabric. In this type of binding, the fabric strip is cut 2" to 2-½"-wide, folded, sewn to the front of the quilt along the edge, folded again, and hand sewn to the quilt back.

Continuous Binding

An easy double-fold binding is "continuous binding with mitered corners" which is applied in one continuous fabric strip with folds turned at each corner to allow extra fabric for a hand-sewn mitered corner. At the joining place, where the binding tails begin and end, a "faux diagonal seam" is created by simply folding a 45-degree angle at the binding's beginning, and tucking into it the cut end of the binding end. The finished binding appears to have only diagonally pieced seams.

Piecing Binding

For continuous binding, the 2-¼" binding strips that you've cut for your quilt need to be sewn together into one long strip. The strip should be longer than the entire circumference of your quilt to allow for piecing the fabric strips with diagonal seam allowances and mitering the four corners.

what if:

If you're short on binding fabric, or simply prefer a single layer of fabric around the edges of your quilt, you can make single-fold binding. Cut these strips narrower and don't fold the strip before sewing it to the quilt. Single-fold binding is appropriate for decorative quilts or wall hangings that won't be handled regularly.

1. To sew the binding strips into one long continuous strip: Place a binding strip vertically, right side up on the work surface. To the left and perpendicular to the vertical strip, lay another binding strip right side down on top of the vertical strip as shown in Photo 1. A catchy way to remember this step is to use the phrase: "ho-down." Place the horizontal strip face down on top of the vertical strip that has already been placed face up on the work surface.

Position binding strips to mark and sew them together using the catch-phrase "ho-down," by placing the horizontal strip face down on top of the vertical strip that's face up.

2. Use a ruler to draw a diagonal line from corner to corner, across the overlapping areas. Because you're marking on the wrong side of the fabric, you can use a pencil since the line will be on the inside. Sew the binding strips together on the drawn line to create a diagonal seam as shown in Photo 2. Repeat to join cut binding strips into one long continuous strip. Trim away the excess fabric and seam allowance to measure ¼".

Sew the binding strips together on the drawn line to create a diagonal seam.

3. Press the sewn seam open to help reduce the bulk as shown in Photo 3.

Press open the trimmed seam.

4

Press a 45-degree diagonal fold at the beginning end of the binding strip.

4. Fold the starting end of the binding at a 45 degree angle as shown in Photo 4; press. This creates the "faux diagonal seam" that gives the binding the illusion of having no stopping or starting point.

5

With wrong sides together, fold and press the entire length of the binding strip.

5. Fold the length of the binding with wrong sides together as shown in Photo 5; press.

Marking the Binding

If you don't have a ¼" foot, draw a line ¼" from the cut edge of the binding. Because the backing and batting extend beyond the raw edge of the quilt top, you won't be able to follow a ¼" guide.

If you don't have a ¼" foot, mark a ¼" line on the binding. Stitch on this line to sew the binding to the quilt.

Sewing the Binding

1. The unbound edges of your quilt will not be straight, and may even be wavy or distorted, perhaps due to quilting or uneven block sizes. Use the long ruler and a water erasable marker or chalk to draw a straight line along the edges of the quilt top.

With a ruler and marker, draw a straight line around the perimeter of the quilt top that will be used as a guide for sewing binding to the quilt edge.

Mark ¼" from both edges in each corner of the quilt top. This point is where your stitching should stop—to then fold and continue sewing to form a mitered corner.

2. Also place a mark ¼" on the inside of all four corners of your quilt as shown in Photo 2. These marks indicate where to stop stitching, fold, and sew the mitered corner.

Pin binding to the quilt as desired. Begin sewing at the top of the diagonal fold.

3. Place the cut edge of the binding strip along the drawn line. Position the binding tail down approximately ¼ from the bottom of the right edge of the quilt. Pin into place. Continue to use pins as desired to secure the binding. Sew the binding on the line that is ¼" from the line marked on the quilt. Begin sewing at the top of the diagonal fold.

TIP: *As you sew, be careful to remove pins as you machine quilt. Attempting to sew over a pin may break the sewing machine needle.*

4. Sew corner to corner, stopping stitches at the ¼" mark as shown in Photo 4. Backstitch; remove the quilt from beneath the presser foot. Snip the threads.

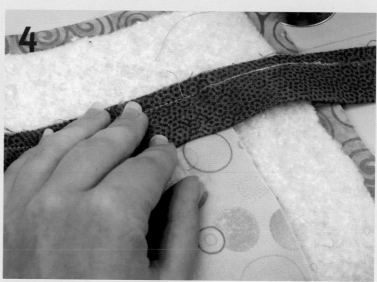

Sew to the ¼" mark on the quilt top. Backstitch.

5. Fold the binding upward to create a 45-degree angle fold as shown in Photo 5. Vertically align the raw edge of the binding with the drawn line.

The upward, 45-degree angle fold.

Bring the binding strip downward to create a horizontal fold. The 45-degree angle fold is hidden underneath.

6. Hold the angle fold and bring the binding strip downward to create a fold that aligns with the drawn line on the top edge.

Begin sewing at the top of the horizontal fold; backstitch.

7. Place the quilt and binding under the presser foot. Begin sewing at the fold, securing stitches with backstitching. Continue pinning and sewing the binding to the quilt, treating each corner in the same manner.

Making a Joining

1. When the needle is at the top diagonal fold (where the stitching began), stop sewing with the needle down as shown in Photo 1. Lay the loose binding end over the diagonal fold. At the point where the binding matches the lower side of the diagonal fold, make a straight cut to remove the remaining binding end.

At the point where the binding meets the lower diagonal fold, trim away the tail end of the binding.

2. Tuck the binding tail into the diagonal fold and continue sewing on top of the beginning stitches as shown in Photo 2. Remove the quilt from the sewing machine.

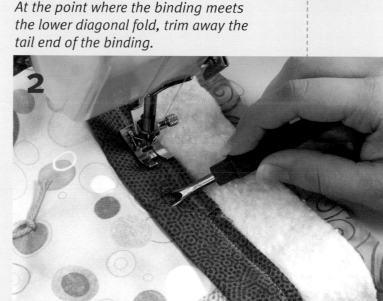

Use the point of a seam ripper to tuck the binding tail into the diagonal fold. Continue sewing to secure the tail and on top of the beginning stitches.

what if:

If you accidentally cut through a sewn corner, there's no quick fix. Remove the binding from the corner and insert a new piece of fabric, sewing diagonal seams to join the strips. Sew the binding to the quilt top.

1

Remove the excess batting and backing from all four sides of the quilt, being careful not to cut into the mitered corner fold.

Trimming the Sandwich

1. On a rotary cutter mat, and with the binding on top, measure ⅜" from the binding stitching line with the long rotary ruler. Rotary cut along the ruler to remove all but ⅜" of the backing and batting as shown in Photo 1. After the binding has been machine sewn to the quilt, cut away the excess fabric and batting. Exercise caution! Be sure to cut away only the excess—not the folded binding or the binding corners.

Adding the Sleeve

Now is the time to add a sleeve for hanging your quilt on the wall (also known as a rod pocket), if desired, Turn to page 100 and follow the instructions before sewing binding onto your quilt. You can simultaneously machine sew the sleeve and binding to the quilt.

1

Turn the folded edge of the binding to the quilt back, aligning the fold with the machine stitches. Use metal hairclips—not straight pins!—to hold the binding in place.

Hand Sewing the Binding

1. After trimming away the excess material on the quilt edge, you're ready to hand sew the binding into place. Lay the quilt on your lap with the backing facing up. Fold the binding to the back. At intervals, clip the binding in place with metal hairclips as shown in Photo 1. They will temporarily hold the binding, and you won't be pricked by the point of straight pins.

2. Take care at each corner to fold and tuck fabric into a diagonal seam as shown in Photo 2. When the binding and four corners have been sewn on the quilt back, turn the quilt over to hand sew each corner mitered seam on the top.

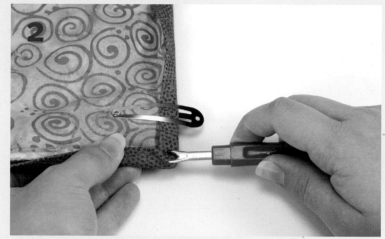

Make sure the binding is tucked into a fold to form a 45-degree mitered corner.

Choosing Binding Thread

For hand-sewing the binding, use a double-strand of thread to give your hand stitches extra strength. Or, use a thread that's a slightly heavier weight than the thread used to piece the quilt. For example, if you used a 50-weight piecing thread, use a 40-weight thread for binding.

Mitered corners on the front and back of the quilt should look the same.

SEWING A SLIP STITCH

Choose a thread color that blends with the binding color.

Knot one end of thread. Begin hand sewing at any point. Stitching from right to left, sew a slip-stitch by hand. Stitches should be ¼" to ⅜" apart. Only a small indent of thread should show.

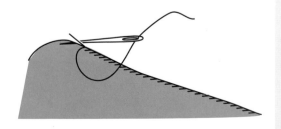

what you need to know about adding a sleeve

If you choose to display your quilt as a wallhanging, the best time to add a sleeve or rod pocket to the quilt is at the same time that binding is sewn to the quilt (see page 98). These instructions are for an "invisible" mounting—when the quilt is hung on the wall, nothing is visible except the quilt.

A wooden yardstick, a piece of drilled hardwood, a medium diameter dowel rod with eyescrews, and a small diameter dowel rod are useful as sleeve rods for the quilts featured in this book.

Choosing the Support

For the quilts in this book choose from a wooden yardstick, a dowel, or a flat board in widths or sizes that support the weight of the quilt to use as the foundation for hanging the quilt on the wall.

To use a wooden yardstick as a sleeve rod, measure and cut a length that will extend 1/2" beyond the finished length of each end of the sleeve. For a mounting that lays flat on the wall, choose a 1" to 2"-wide board.

A ½" to ⅝" diameter wooden dowel is a good size, or for very small quilts, choose a wooden dowel rod with a small diameter. Avoid using any large diameter dowel rod—wooden or metal—because it may not lay flat against the wall.

Adding the Sleeve

1. Make a sleeve from the same fabric as your quilt backing. The sleeve won't be obvious, especially if you decide to use the quilt instead of displaying it on a wall.

2. Measure the top of the quilt and add 5". This measurement allows a 1 ½" fold at each sleeve end and for centering the sleeve 1" in from each edge of the quilt back to make sure it doesn't show from the front when you hang the quilt .

3. Because the finished width of the sleeve is a double fold, cut a strip of fabric that is 8" wide by the width of the quilt top, plus 5".

4. At each end of the sleeve make a 1 ½" fold to the wrong side. Press.

5. Fold the sleeve length in half, wrong sides together. Press.

Unfinished sleeve width = 8"

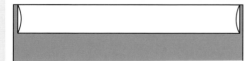

Unfinished sleeve length = Quilt width plus 5"

6. Align the raw edges of the sleeve with the top, trimmed, raw edge of the quilt back, centering the sleeve 1" in from each edge of the quilt back. Pin in place.

7. Lengthen your sewing machine stitch to machine baste the sleeve to the quilt, using a scant ¼" seam.

8. By hand, slip stitch the binding to the back of the quilt. Then sew the folded edge of the sleeve to the quilt backing, making sure not to take stitches that will show on the quilt front.

Align the raw edges of the folded sleeve with the raw edges of the quilt top; pin. Be sure the binding is tucked completely out of the way before sewing the sleeve into place.

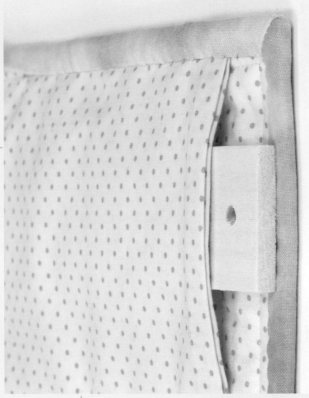

The sleeve is slip-stitched to the quilt back. The hardwood board is drilled, so the quilt is ready to hang.

Preparing for Display

1. Deduct 1" from the measurement of the quilt top and cut a yardstick or a 1" to 2-½"-wide, flat board that length.

2. Approximately ⅓" from each end of the yardstick or board, drill a hole that will accommodate a finishing nail head.

3. Position the board on the wall and mark the location of the drilled holes.

4. Hammer nails through these marks.

5. Insert the drilled board through the sleeve.

With a mounting like this, the hardwood board and nail are hidden by the quilt.

Displaying the Quilt

1. Position the yardstick or board on the nails to hang the quilt.

2. If you're using a dowel rod with eyescrews to hang the quilt, position the eyescrews on the finishing nails. Or, for a smaller dowel, simply rest the ends of the dowel across the nails.

Creating a Label

Personalize your quilt with a label that includes:

- your name
- city and state
- month and year

If you are making the quilt to give as a gift, additional information can include:

- the reason for which the quilt was given
- the name of the quilt recipient
- any special thoughts or a poem
- a photo

Labeling Options

There are many easy methods for creating inexpensive but visually attractive labels:

- Handwriting on a pre-printed fabric label or directly onto the quilt front or back
- Embroidering a label by machine or by hand
- Printing using your computer's software to design a label. Then print it from your color printer onto prepared fabric that's been backed with paper. Follow the manufacturer's instructions for best results.

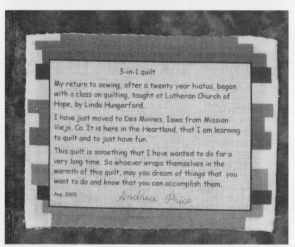

glossary of quiltmaking terms

Appliqué The sewing technique for attaching pieces (appliqués) of fabric onto a background fabric. Appliqués may be stitched to the background by hand, using a blind stitch, or by machine, using a satin stitch or a blind hemstitch.

Basting The sewing technique for joining layers of fabric or the layers of a quilt with safety pins or large stitches. The stitching is temporary and is removed after permanent stitching. Pin-basting is accomplished using small safety pins to temporarily hold layers together.

Batting A layer of filler placed between two pieces of fabric to form a quilt. Its thickness and fiber content varies.

Bias The grain of woven fabric that is at a 45-degree angle to the selvages.

Binding The strip of fabric used to cover the outside edges—top, batting and backing—of a quilt.

Block A basic unit of a quilt top.

Border A strip of fabric that is joined to the inner quilt, or quilt center, to enhance it.

Chain-piecing or Chaining The action of sewing a pair of fabric pieces together and continuously pushing pairs under the presser foot without cutting the thread between them.

Cornerstone A fabric square positioned at the corner of sashing strips, or a plain square or pieced block used in the four corners of a quilt border.

Echo quilting A type of outline quilting in which the first line of quilting is quilted in-the-ditch of an appliqué motif. The next line is quilted a measurement (i.e. ½") away from the first, and subsequent lines ½" from previous lines.

Finger-pressing A method for forming temporary guidelines by pressing fabric between your fingers to make a temporary crease.

Finished size The measurement of a completed block that has been sewn into a quilt.

Fat Quarter A one yard length of fabric that has been cut into four equal rectangles each measuring approximately 18 x 20".

Grain The direction of woven fabric. The cross grain is from selvage to selvage. The lengthwise grain runs parallel to the selvage and is stronger. The bias grain is at a 45- degree angle and has the greatest amount of stretch.

In-the-ditch quilting The top stitching that is made alongside a seam, usually on the side without the seam allowance.

Mitered seam A 45-degree angle seam.

Outline quilting Stitching that is made outside or inside the pieced seamlines of patchwork.

Patchwork A composite of pieces sewn together to form a larger piece, such as a quilt.

Pressing Using an iron with an up and down motion to set stitches and flatten a seam allowance, usually pressed toward the darker fabric.

Quilting The small running stitches made through the layers of a quilt (quilt top, batting and backing) to form decorative patterns on the surface of the quilt and hold the layers together.

Quilting thread A heavy cotton thread used for hand-quilting.

Rotary-cutting The process of cutting fabric into strips and pieces using a revolving blade rotary cutter, a thick, clear plastic ruler, and a special cutting mat.

Raw edge The cut end of fabric.

Seam allowance The ¼" margin of fabric between the stitched seam and the raw edge.

Seam line The guideline that the quilter follows while stitching.

Selvage The lengthwise finished edge on each side of the fabric.

Set or setting The arrangement of blocks in a quilt top.

Setting square A plain block that's sewn next to a pieced block.

Sleeve A fabric "tunnel" that is sewn to the top edge of the quilt back. It is also called a rod pocket and used with a board or rod as a support to hang a quilt on the wall.

Slipstitch A hand-stitch used for finishing such as sewing binding to a quilt, or a sleeve to a quilt back.

Strip-sets Two or more strips of fabric, cut and sewn together along the length of the strips.

Sub-cut Cutting fabric strip sets into smaller units.

Unfinished size The measurement of a block or quilt before the ¼" seam allowance is sewn.

introducing first-time quiltmakers

Designs for the four quilts featured in Lesson Four of this book were developed by Linda Hungerford, project editor, teaching first-time quiltmakers in Stitchin' Mission™, a series of beginning quiltmaking classes taught regularly at Lutheran Church of Hope in West Des Moines, Iowa.

Stitchin' Mission™ continues today, and its purpose is two-fold: Teach the basics of quiltmaking, and make kids' quilts for Hope's missions. For each class, little or no investment is required by the first-time quiltmaker because the quilts are made for charity with donated tools and fabric.

Each Stitchin' Mission™ class begins with prayers asking God for help in learning to "sew straight stitches." While sewing at home first-time quiltmakers ask for blessings on the child who will receive the quilt.

For Linda, who has been quilting since 1976, her greatest reward as a quilting teacher comes from sharing first-time quiltmaking with students who initially come to class as the biggest skeptics—

feeling sure they will fail. She finds that of her first-time quiltmakers, those with the least confidence are those who inevitably fall the hardest for quilting. However, it's each student's positive attitude that makes quiltmaking do-able. It's wonderful for Linda and her first-time quiltmakers to discover the joys of quiltmaking as they help each other.

Three of the quilt patterns in this book are basic, yet similar, so when taught in the Stitchin' Mission™ class, it's easy to simultaneously make two quilts during six weeks of lessons. This speeds up the learning process especially when the first-time quiltmaker selects two different patterns.

With a little help from her friends, one Stitchin' Mission™ overachiever made nine quilts in six weeks!

As you read through the pages of this book and try making one or all of the featured quilts, it is Linda's desire that you too experience that joy of first-time quiltmaking, and receive the blessing of "straight stitches."

Left to right: Andrea Price, Abigail Livingood, Jackie Svetly, Michelle Tepley, Ann Spencer, Mary Nichols, Susan Murdock, Erika Horstmann, Karaan Vogel, Kathy Martin, Cindy Covey, Julie Miller, Debra Douglas, and instructor Linda Hungerford

gallery

Most of the quilts shown on the following pages were made by first-time quilters, many of whom hadn't sat in front of a sewing machine "since high school"—which for some of them goes back a few years!

As you successfully complete the quilts featured in this book, you may want to consider contributing the quilt you make to a worthwhile organization, as were these Stitchin' Mission™ quilts.

You'll have the pleasure and satisfaction of making your first quilt, and a deserving child will benefit from your gift of time and talent.

four-patch by Donna Wilson

four-patch by Linda Hungerford

single-patch by Ann Spencer

single-patch by Su McCurdy

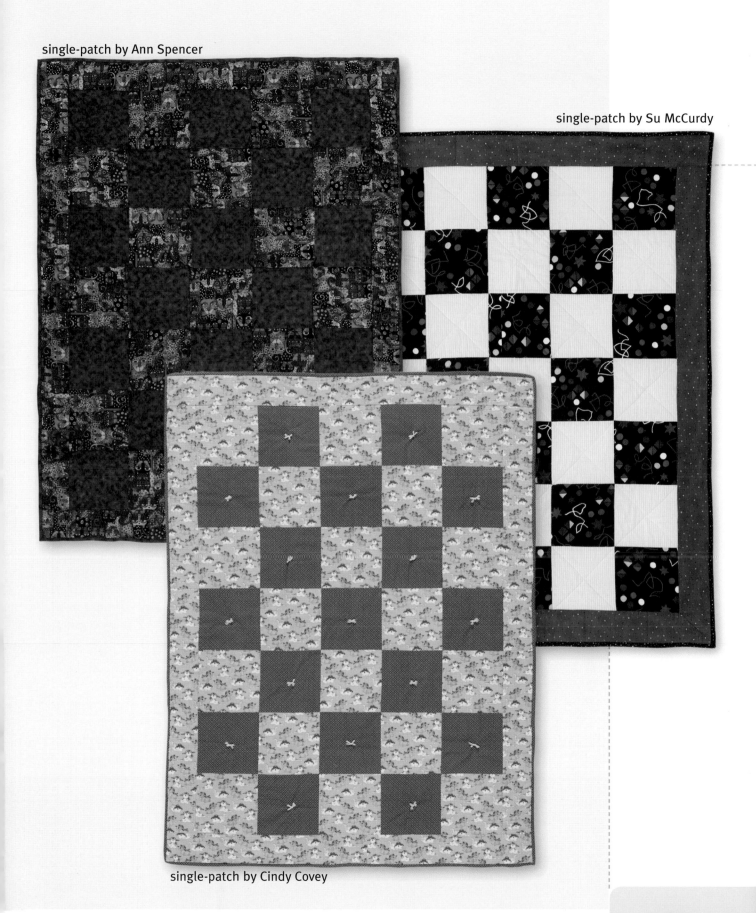

single-patch by Cindy Covey

three-rail by Cathie Conley

three-rail by Donna Wilson

three-rail by Linda Hungerford

three-rail by Mary Nichols